Nurturing Faith in the Family

JFL *Judson Family Life Series*

Nurturing Faith in the Family

Jan and Myron Chartier

Judson Press® Valley Forge

Other Books in the Judson Family Life Series

Help for Remarried Couples and Families
Caught in the Middle: Children of Divorce
Letters to a Retired Couple
The Springtime of Love and Marriage
Live and Learn with Your Teenager
The Church in the Life of the Black Family
Child Rearing in Today's Christian Family
Marriage in the Middle Years

NURTURING FAITH IN THE FAMILY

Copyright © 1986
Judson Press, Valley Forge, PA 19482-0851

Scripture quotations are from the *Good News Bible*, the Bible in Today's English Version. Copyright © American Bible Society, 1976. Used by permission.

Library of Congress Cataloging-in-Publication Data
Chartier, Jan.
  Nurturing faith in the family.

  (Judson family life series)
  Bibliography: p.
  1. Family—Religious life. I. Chartier, Myron
Raymond.   II. Title.   III. Series.
BV4526.2.C43   1986   249   86-2936
ISBN 0-8170-1093-9

Dedicated to

our daughter, Mel
and
our son, Tim

who have participated alongside us
in our attempts to create a
meaningful family faith portrait
with both broad and fine strokes.

Contents

Foreword

Nurturing Faith in the Family is the editors' contribution to the Judson Family Life Series. At a meeting of various marriage and family life specialists discussing ideas and concerns about volumes to be included in such a series, one member of the group felt strongly that a separate book on faith nurturing in the family should be included. His suggestion received strong support from those present.

This book became for us a challenge to sort out and express in words our approaches and convictions about faith nurturing in the family. As the ideas came together, the chapters emerged and a book manuscript took shape.

Throughout this book readers will encounter case materials. Those from our own family life record the events as we perceived them to happen. In other case studies we have made alterations to protect confidentiality, yet we have attempted to preserve the accuracy of the human dynamics involved. In our research we discovered a number of persons, couples, and/or families who could say of our descriptions of different family situations ''There we are. That case fits us!'' We hope in such instances our readers realize that ''one case fits many.''

Our book is one of a series of volumes being published by Judson Press on marriage and family for contemporary Christians. The purposes of the Judson Family Life Series are to inform, educate, and enrich Christian persons and inspire them—

 a. to become acquainted with the complex dynamics of marriage and family living;

b. to pinpoint those attitudes, behavioral skills, and processes which nurture health and wholeness in relationships rather than sickness and fragmentation;

c. to consider marriage and family today in light of the Judeo-Christian faith.

As editors of Judson Family Life Series, we have been committed to making available the latest in family-life theory and research and to helping Christian families discover pathways to wholeness in relationships. Every attempt has been made by the authors to apply new insights to the realities of daily living in marriage and the family.

Other volumes in the series focus on the stages of marriage, divorce and remarriage, parenting, and the black family. Each is designed to deal with specific issues in marriage and family living today.

We want to take this opportunity to thank Harold Twiss, former general manager of Judson Press, who opened the door for us to edit this series. Following his resignation from Judson Press, senior editor Phyllis Frantz assumed overall responsibilities for the series in mid-development. We are appreciative to her and others on the staff for assisting us in that transition.

Finally, we are deeply grateful to our Eastern Baptist Theological Seminary friends (board of directors, administration, and faculty colleagues) for granting us sabbatical leave together and, thereby, lightening our load to provide for unburdened writing time. Having both of us on sabbatical has meant added responsibilities for many seminary colleagues. We are grateful for their support and for their confidence that we would, indeed, complete this volume entitled *Nurturing Faith in the Family.*

Jan and Myron Chartier
The Eastern Baptist Theological Seminary
Philadelphia, Pennsylvania

PART ONE
The Challenge of and Commitment to Faith Nurturing in the Family

The Challenge of
Faith Nurturing

We have been married for twenty-six years. Over the years we certainly have had our share of joys and blessings, but we have also had our share of hardships. We have dealt with the death of parents and grandparents and have faced economic hardships. Three out of four members of our family have had their turn in the hospital. Three of us have chronic health problems that need constant care and attention through proper rest, good diet, and appropriate exercise. Two of us have had to cope with life-threatening illnesses. We have had to deal with the stress of moves and the necessary readjustments.

As we look at what other families have had to face, our difficulties, though real, seem small. Families we know have lost members through illness or accidents. The primary breadwinners in some families have lost their jobs. Other families have had to deal with teenagers who have had babies out of wedlock or who have sought abortions. Others have had to struggle with daughters and sons who have become addicted to drugs or convicted by the law. Still others have seen the breakup of their family through separation and divorce.

On the first page of his best-selling book *The Road Less Traveled,* M. Scott Peck confronts the reader with these startling statements: ''Life is difficult. . . . Life is a series of problems.'' [1] How do we cope with life in our families amidst the difficulties of life in general and in our families specifically? Some difficulties arise from the normal transitions of life—such as children growing up and parents getting older. Other difficulties are catastrophic—the family farm is taken by the bank because of the inability to pay the mortgage, the family home is destroyed by a tornado, or a family member becomes paralyzed below the neck from an auto accident.

Faith and Family Coping

How are we to face the struggles of family living? People have to find ways to cope in order to find strength to go on living. We have known families who have overindulged in alcoholic beverages, become despairing, or have given up on their marriages and families when they have been faced by life's tragedies. However, we, like many other families over the years, have found our trust in God to be an undergirding, sustaining power. Our faith has given us hope and strength as we have faced each day. Some of our life circumstances could have led us to despair and family breakup if it had not been for the resources of our common faith in God.

Family research has shown that families use religious beliefs and practices as a fundamental coping strategy for dealing with the stresses and strains of life.[2] The importance of faith in families was highlighted in a recent study conducted by the University of Minnesota through its Department of Family Social Sciences.[3] In 1981 members of this department involved 1,140 families from thirty-one states in a groundbreaking study of what makes families work.

In their study they sought to understand the dynamics of family coping. They identified five basic coping strategies that families use in the face of difficulty. Their study showed that "seeking spiritual support" was the most important overall coping strategy for the families.

How does religious faith help families cope with the stresses and strains of life? According to the Minnesota researchers religious faith is critical in managing long separation in families. Faith is important in maintaining the family unit and in bolstering personal self-esteem. They also think that religious faith provides an important social plumbline for guiding families through stressful and socially ambiguous situations. Religious faith is an essential ingredient in coming to terms with the difficulties of family living.

Faith and Healthy Families

Given the results of the University of Minnesota research on family coping strategies, it should come as no surprise that religious faith is important to family health. A number of research studies have found that strong, healthy families are religious families.[4]

Through their Family Strengths Research Project, the Department of

Human Development and the Family at the University of Nebraska has conducted several of these studies. Their investigation began with 130 strong families in Oklahoma and was later expanded to a national study that included urban and rural families. Later studies included South American and Russian immigrant families as well as families from many other ethnic backgrounds—Blacks, Poles, Jews, Italians, and Hispanics.[5]

Through these studies the Family Strengths Research Project discovered six qualities that characterize strong families. Among these was a high degree of religious orientation. There are, of course, persons who are not religious but have happy marriages and good family relationships. Nevertheless, marriage and family research over the past forty years has shown a positive relationship between religious faith, marital happiness, and good family relationships.

Strong families tend to be quite religious. Although not all belong to an organized church, they attend church services together and regularly participate in religious activities such as family prayer and Bible reading.

For strong families religious faith goes beyond beliefs and attending religious services to a commitment to a spiritual lifestyle that is practical and interpersonal. They have an awareness of God as a higher power that provides them with a sense of purpose, meaning, and fulfillment as well as support and strength for their families. Strong families find that a sensitivity to God in their daily lives helps them to be patient with each other, less petty, more forgiving, quicker to get over anger, and more positive and supportive in their relationships with one another.[6] Certainly when the values of Christian faith are put into day-to-day action they greatly enrich the quality of our life together as families.

Faith Nurturing and the Family

Research studies have demonstrated the importance of religious faith on coping in healthy families. How do families develop faith? Where does it come from?

There is a serious question as to whether or not faith can be taught apart from the family. Much of faith is taught not only through the spoken word but through living within the context of family and neighbors. Christian faith involves a trust in God through Jesus Christ that impacts thought, emotion, conduct, and relationships.[7]

A trusting relationship with God affects a person's whole existence. The family is still the primary unit in our society for conveying faith in positive and meaningful ways. Other organizations can provide important support, but if the family fails in the task of nurturing faith, persons of the future may lack an abiding faith in Jesus Christ as the center and focus of their lives.

Findings from Research

The importance of what we are saying is pointed up by some research findings gathered by sociologist James Krile of the University of Minnesota. He says, "If you are a kid who grew up in a family that went to church, you're more apt to go to church. . . . this is especially true if the father went to church." [8] He concludes from his findings that if the father doesn't attend services, neither are his children likely to do so. His findings indicate that parental modeling is the most powerful single influence upon children's faith development. Such parental influence cannot be taught in the Sunday church school or the parochial school. The influence of parental modeling upon children's faith nurturing goes far beyond impacting their future church attendance. It also affects beliefs, values, and lifestyle.

A Biblical Model for Faith Nurturing

A basic model for religious nurturing is found in ancient Israel, where faith was passed on from one generation to the next in the midst of daily family living.

> Israel, remember this! The LORD—and the LORD alone—is our God. Love the LORD your God with all your heart, with all your soul, and with all your strength. Never forget these commands that I am giving you today. Teach them to your children. Repeat them when you are at home and when you are away, when you are resting and when you are working. Tie them on your arms and wear them on your foreheads as a reminder. Write them on the doorposts of your houses and on your gates (Deuteronomy 6:4-9, TEV).

Israel was to love God by being obedient to the Lord's commandments and by imparting the faith to the children of succeeding generations. As a result an attitude of love and obedience among the people of God would be maintained from age to age. Deuteronomy attaches an importance to nurturing faith in the family. The ways of God are to be a topic for conversation at all times. Israel's families were to teach faith in God through the whole of life. Both God's love and the covenant obligations were to be the central and absorbing interest of family living.

When children asked about their religious traditions, the parents would reply, ''Once we were slaves in Egypt, but the Lord delivered us from bondage. Our God called Moses to be our leader and brought us out of the land of Egypt by taking us through the Red Sea, over the desert, and to the mountain. There the Lord made a covenant with us and made us the people of God. Then this God led us through the wilderness for forty years and finally brought us over the Jordan River into this land which is now our home.''

What a tremendous recital of the history of God's people! The story of the Israelite people gave the next generation a faith identity and destiny.

There are many occasions for introducing children to the great words, concepts, and stories of the Christian gospel in daily family living. Children raise many questions that relate to the essence of faith. Their questions emerge from conversations they hear, books they read, television programs they watch, and crises they experience. The family provides a context for both parents, and children to explore the depths of faith. Parents, even theologically trained ones, can be hard pressed at times to come up with cogent responses to their children's questions.

The Family and the Church

In ancient Israel there was an integral relationship between the family and the larger faith community. Indeed, the nation saw itself as a large family. The same can be said for the Christian church. There is an intricate relationship between the family and the church. This relationship has long been recognized within the church. The apostle Paul used ''family'' as a key metaphor for thinking about the church as community. God is our loving parent; Jesus Christ is our elder brother, and we are brothers and sisters in Christ. The family has been viewed as a little church by John Chrysostom of the Patristic period and Martin Luther of the Protestant Reformation. Whenever family members commit their family life to God, a community of faith exists. Within their relationships the life of faith is shaped and lived. The family is a primary relational unit in God's family, the church.

The family as a microcommunity of faith performs many nurturing functions that are needed in the family of God. If the church is to be strong and serve God's purpose in the world, it needs strong families that nurture its members in belonging, being, believing, benefiting, and becoming.

Belonging

One cannot be human alone. We exist through our "we" relationships. One of the challenges of faith nurturing in the Christian family is to help growing persons, young and old alike, learn to communicate with one another, hear and be heard, forgive and be forgiven, accept and be accepted, love and be loved; in short, to belong and feel secure in that belonging. By being a part of a family, human beings are in a context in which they can experience, learn, and express caring. Like the church, the Christian family is called to be a caring community. It is in caring relationships that we know we belong and can help others know that they belong.

Being

Within the context of family interaction an "I" emerges. There is no such thing as identity apart from relationships with others; and for the growing child the family is critical to the process of an emerging being. Identity with all the powers of thinking, feeling, and acting is shaped within the context of family living. The uniquely personal powers of exploring, choosing, solving problems, influencing, and competing are first learned in the family. These powers are further shaped, refined, and reinforced as we interact with marital partners and with children. Helping family members discover their own unique being is one of the challenges for faith nurturing in the family.

Believing

The need for meaning is unique to human beings. We are haunted by such questions as "What is the meaning of life? What is the meaning of my life? Why were we put here? What do we live for? What shall we live by? If we must die, if nothing endures, then what sense does anything make?" Believing is important to meaning. Our Judeo-Christian faith provides a system of thought that answers some of these basic life questions. Therefore, another challenge for faith nurturing in the family is to learn the language of faith. The verbal and nonverbal symbols of Christian faith need to be part of the everyday experience of family living. Such experiences provide the basis for family members to work out the meaning of life under God.

Benefiting

Ultimately the family needs to find its mission in God's world. A family that lives only for itself has become an idol unto itself. God's family lives to benefit the world through Christian love and service. It has the challenging responsibility of nurturing its members to be God's agents in the world by meeting the needs of persons, by reconciling alienated individuals and groups, and by transforming the structures and conditions of society. Faith nurturing in the family helps its members in benefiting others.

Becoming

Family members are always in the process of development. The baby is moving toward childhood; the young mother is moving toward middle age; the grandfather is moving toward his eternal home. We are in the process of becoming; we are never complete until death comes. In our process of becoming, our sense of belonging changes as new members enter our family, as we leave our family of origin to marry and form our own family, and as our children leave home to marry and have children that are our grandchildren. Our sense of being, our identity, is in a process of change as we move through the various life stages. Our believing changes as new meanings are needed for new life experiences. Our methods of benefiting others also change as we move through life's stages and encounter new interpersonal and social problems. Faith nurturing in the family meets this challenge by helping its members encounter these changes and important life processes.

A Concluding Word

Faith nurturing within the family is important for basically two reasons. First, healthy, coping families have a high degree of religious orientation. Second, the family as an integral part of the church has an important task in nurturing its members in faith. These two reasons provide the challenge for nurturing faith through the families of our society.

Questions for Reflection and Discussion

1. In what ways can you confirm from your own experience (or from those you know) the statement that "life is difficult"?

2. What are some of the ways your family has coped with hard times? What has been the place of faith?

3. In what ways has your faith been shaped by parental modeling? In what ways was the faith modeling in your home similar to or different

from that described in Deuteronomy 6:4-9?

4. What insights have you gained from the idea that the family is "a little church" or a microcommunity of faith?

5. To what extent have you taken seriously the idea that God is your loving parent, Jesus is your elder brother, and other Christians are your brothers and sisters in Christ?

2

Commitment to Faith Nurturing

If religious families who live out their faith are healthier and cope with crisis more successfully, logic would indicate that nearly every family would place a high priority on nurturing a dynamic faith in and among its members. They would work to make that growth happen. They would seek to keep their faith vital and strong. They would be committed to faith nurturing.

Unfortunately this kind of dedication to faith growth is frequently not the case in family living. Many families give little or no attention to faith nurturing. Others express the desire for faith nurturing, but they assume it will simply happen without significant investment. We have heard numerous case histories from students we have worked with over the last twenty years which confirm this picture.

One young man reported, ''I was baptized a Roman Catholic, but we never went to church. We never talked about God or religious things in our home. I don't think we owned a Bible. I was converted when I was in college. A whole new world opened up for me. I found out there was so much more to life than making money, getting ahead, and watching television.'' This young man had married a woman from a Christian home. He described the contrast between the two homes as ''unbelievable.''

A middle-aged woman entered seminary after a painful divorce. She described her marriage as one in which faith in God meant nothing. Meaning for the whole family was determined by her husband's climb to a high-status executive position. Their children, now young adults, had hardly known their father. He had provided them with abundant material possessions, but rarely did he give them his presence. "It all finally fell apart. The divorce was ugly. Then it ended. I was all alone. When I reached the bottom of the pit, I met God face to face. Now I know what faith is."

A college student in one of Jan's classes wrote a paper beginning with her deepest wish that she could have a family who cared for her as a person. She believed her parents had sent her to a boarding high school because they had no time for her. Now they had sent her two thousand miles away to college. She had flown home for a debutante party. "The whole thing was engineered by my parents. It was as if I didn't exist. Now I'm back here trying to figure out why I am in college anyway." The paper ended with a paragraph weighing the possibility of suicide. During the remaining weeks she was in Jan's class, the two of them had some extended conversations. Jan learned that social status, money, and achievement were important in that family. Religious faith seemed to be totally irrelevant even though the parents were nominal members of the most prestigious church in town.

Just as these stories remind us that many families do not give attention to religious faith, other stories demonstrate how faith nurtured in the family has sustained persons and given them purpose. These stories include economic hardship, death of a parent, physical handicaps, divorces, serious illness, and natural disasters. In every case their faith provided them with the resources to continue coping with life. As we listened to those kinds of life histories and thought about our own upbringing in families where faith and values were taken seriously, we became aware that these families had worked at being faithful people. It didn't happen automatically. These people invested time and energy in faith nurturing, and they knew what it meant to each family member. Although most of those families would probably not talk about their relationship to their faith in these terms, we want to label them as "committed faith nurturers." The Christian faith was central in their lives. Life's meaning was rooted in their identities as Christians. They worked at being Christian.

If families are to commit themselves to faith nurturing, we believe that they need perspective on God's covenantal love for humanity and the world as well as awareness of the need for commitment to faith nurturing in the marriage, in parenting, and in the family as a whole unit. Faith nurturing is more likely to happen if the church and its families share in mutual commitment to undergird the faith nurturing process.

Formulating a Faith-Nurturing Framework

Families who are serious about meaningful faith nurturing need to develop a focus as to what such a task is attempting to accomplish. Reasons for faith nurturing such as "the church expects it" or "our families of origin engaged in some faith-nurturing practices" are insufficient for establishing solid faith-nurturing approaches. The formulation of a framework that contains the core of the Christian faith can serve as a basis and guide. Without such a framework faith nurturing is likely to be haphazard and may be reduced primarily to techniques. Developing such a guiding framework and core requires serious biblical study and theological reflection.

In answering the question "What is the Christian faith?" H. Richard Niebuhr, the renowned theologian and ethicist, once wrote "to love God and neighbor."[1] Karl Barth, the distinguished Swiss theologian, wrote his many-volumed *Church Dogmatics* and thereby responded to that question in great detail. Our response is longer than Niebuhr's sentence, but far less extensive than Barth's volumes. In the following section we will share the core of the framework we have developed for faith nurturing in our family. We will identify some key theological themes which seem to us to highlight the basis from which Christians in their response to the living God commit themselves to faith growth in their personal lives as well as in their families. You, as the reader, should feel free to spend time adding your own theological understandings to the core we have written.

A Core Statement of the Christian Faith

We love because God first loved us. We are faithful in our relationships with others because God has been faithful to us. We forgive others because God has forgiven us.

These profound theological truths grow from our understanding of the core of what the Christian faith is all about. The living God invested creative power to bring the whole of creation into existence. Humanity as male and female are the crown of creation. Human beings are made for giving glory to God through love, praise, responsibility, and obedient relationship. God intends that they live interdependently in balanced, loving relationships, supporting one another in the process of becoming all that God intends them to be.

Love can be genuine only if it is freely given. God created man and woman with freedom. They are free to choose to love—to love God and each other. Freedom involves being choice makers at every turn of life. Every human faces countless choices.

Through creation, the gift of life, and the possibility of loving relationships God said yes to humanity. In the beginning humanity said yes to God. Yes to life and breath. Yes to each other. Yes to stewardship of God's creation. Eventually humanity decided to explore the possibility of saying no. They ate the forbidden fruit. Woman and man chose their way over God's way. The consequences were beyond anything they could have imagined. Distance from God, loneliness, alienation, condemnation, guilt, suspicion, deceit, drunkenness, jealousy, and murder became woven into life's broken structure. Man and woman had to struggle to be choice makers. Questions flooded their choice-making process. Yes? No? Maybe? What will our choice mean? There is no longer a clear way. Even our yes to God and to each other is clouded with a tinge of no. Can we return to where we once were? Will we ever again be able to say a clear, definitive yes! to God? What are we to do? Our attempts to reestablish our relationship to God seem so hopeless. There is nothing we can do. Despair is all around.

In the midst of humanity's despair, the living God was present to love faithfully regardless of humanity's yes/no/maybe uncertainties. God did not abandon humanity or the world. The loving God was constantly available to hear, to forgive, to call, to lead, to protect, and to deliver. The God who had created humanity for love had continued to say ''yes!'' God's word was faithful and true.

In time humanity began to realize that the living God was personal and had created human beings to be covenant partners living in trust and obedience to God's purpose. The people of Israel became the light so others could see. Their identity was defined by the God who said, ''I will be your God and you will be my people. I will be your God to protect you and to deliver you, to call and to guide you, to love and to forgive you.''

''My people are to live in trust and obedience. You are to trust me and I will be there for you. I will sustain you according to my will. You are to wait confidently and hopefully. You are to listen to my voice and follow my leading'' (authors' paraphrase of Old Testament content).

Humanity found trusting and obedient living very difficult. The attitudes required seemed to go against human inclinations to be powerful and in control. Humanity continued to go its own way, showing unfaithfulness to God. In each situation a great leader, a prophetic voice, a disastrous exile, a redemptive deliverance called humanity to account.

They gained some awareness of what they had done. They turned and changed their ways. However, the cycle repeated itself again and again.

Finally, the voice of the prophet Jeremiah spoke God's words, "The time is coming when I will make a new covenant with the people of Israel and the people of Judah. . . . The new covenant that I will make will be this. I will put my law within them and write it on their hearts. They will all know me. I will be their God. I will forgive their sins. They will be my people" (Jeremiah 31:31-34, authors' paraphrase).

When the time was right, a baby was born and he was named Jesus. He grew up in a family. His baptism by John the Baptist signaled the beginning of his ministry. Jesus taught and healed the sick. He preached and interpreted Scripture. He confronted the religious leaders who no longer had a clear picture of what it meant to be God's people. He nurtured the disciples in understanding that he was God's Son and that those who would see and hear would see the living God through the Son. He promised the coming of the Holy Spirit in a new way to God's people. He was crucified and buried.

When Jesus died, again all seemed hopeless. Despair engulfed his followers. All they had hoped for seemed to have evaporated before them. But on the third day Jesus Christ rose and conquered death. The resurrection provided for a new covenant, a new day, and a new way of being God's people!

Jesus told his followers to wait. After a time the Spirit came. The Christian church began. The Spirit moved among the Jews and the Gentiles, drawing them to faith in Jesus Christ.

Over the centuries the Good News of God in Christ spread from continent to continent. As the Good News spread, so did the struggle for God's followers to remain faithful. Humanity continued to face the challenge of being responsible in choosing God's way. Today the inclination to decide to follow our own desires still pervades our daily living.

God continues to remain faithful, having loved the world so much that the only son Jesus was given that all who believe in him might have life and renewed relationship with God and with one another. Today's community of believers is still to live in trust and obedience. However, the "rub" of being human continues within us: we have trouble surrendering everything to our Lord.

Implications of the Core

What are the implications of this theological core for those who are members of the faith community? What can families learn from a consideration of these key theological ideas to guide them in faith nurturing?

Becoming a faith person is a lifelong process. Becoming God's covenant partner is far from an automatic process. The process of nurturing faith must be intentional on the part of believers. We must nurture one another. It is a matter of calling and commitment. The family is a crucial arena for faith nurturing.

God's covenant has endured through the ages. God's love has been faithful and true. We believe that for Christian people there is a covenanting dimension to our relationships. We cannot be God to one another. I can never love another human being as God loves, but my love for that person can reflect a dimension of God's covenantal love. As we mature in life and in faith, we are to become ever more Christlike by conforming ourselves to his personhood and way of being. My relationship with another human being can be a kind of parable which points to God's covenant with humankind. This kind of covenanting dimension should underlie relationships in family living where we are bonded together in a unique way. Relationships which reflect a covenanting dimension are relationships characterized by deep commitment.

Commitment to Faith Nurturing in Marriage

Very little commitment is necessary in marriage ceremonies. Saying the appropriate words is relatively simple.

A couple exchanges rings, gives each other an endearing kiss, marches down the aisle, attends a festive celebration and it's all over! They're married.

Marriage experts have increasingly emphasized that we need to distinguish between the wedding ceremony and the marriage relationship. The ceremony formalizes and legalizes a marriage, but the relationship usually began long before the wedding and will continue to be shaped throughout the duration of the marriage.

Relationships, if they are to be qualitative, if they are to deepen and to grow, require a great deal of investment on the part of the persons involved. Our daughter, in her senior year of college, is in the process of discovering how much work is involved in developing ongoing, rewarding relationships. One afternoon when she was living at home during the summer months she asked her mother in utter frustration, ''Mom, why do relationships have to consume so much time?'' Later in the week she altered her question slightly in a conversation with her father, ''Dad, why do relationships take so much work? Sometimes I wonder if they are worth it!''

During our twenty-six years of marriage we have invested much time and energy into what it means to be ''us''—Myron and Jan relating meaningfully and fairly to each other. The time and energy have not come automatically. We have had to choose to take the time and invest the energies in spite of the pressures of parenting, jobs, friendships, church activities, crises, or extended family.

David Mace has pointed out that in an earlier day when established roles informed men and women, husbands and wives, who they were to be in society and to each other, relationships could survive without as much attention and personal investment.[2] However, times have changed and we no longer live in a society with clearly defined roles for women or for men. We are in a state of flux. Each couple has to negotiate who the husband will be and who the wife will be as individuals and as a team. Such negotiations are delicate and the consequences are far-reaching. To make the task more complex, one series of negotiations will rarely, if ever, settle matters for the rest of the marriage. All kinds of life changes impinge on the relationship and the couple must renegotiate their roles again and again.

Relationships are hard work; they require time and energy. If the relationship is to be meaningful, both persons involved have to commit themselves to relational work as long as the relationship lasts. Such commitment requires an ongoing investment of self. Marriages cannot thrive if relational work is neglected.

There is something profoundly theological about the relational work involved in marriage. To strive for integrity in the covenanting dimension of marriage stands as a lifelong relational challenge. The thoughts of a committed marriage partner forming a theological viewpoint toward marriage might be stated something like this:

''I am a child of God. My spouse is a child of God. We belong to God's family. We are God's children. Our marriage relationship exists within the context of God's family. It must bear the marks which characterize that family.[3]

''I was created uniquely in the image of God. My spouse was created uniquely in the image of God. We are both unique and precious. My needs are no more central than the needs of my spouse. We must learn to cooperate in meeting both of our needs.

''God created me to be a choice maker. My spouse was also created by God to be a choice maker. Because our lives have become intertwined through marriage, the choices I make will affect my spouse. The choices my spouse makes will affect me. Our freedom is interlinked because of our marriage.

"Patterned after God's covenant with humanity, my commitment and my love for my spouse are steadfast and faithful. They endure through time. God's covenant was enduring from age to age in all kinds of historical settings. Just so must our love and commitment endure through time."

When married partners cannot or choose not to be all that they had hoped to be to each other, pain enters that relationship. Such pain tears at the trust fabric of the relationship. There is brokenness between the two people. At those times God's covenant with humankind stands as a relational road map to help persons understand that forgiveness is the process through which the relationship is restored. God's gracious forgiveness of us frees us to forgive one another.[4]

Sometimes pain and negative dynamics become so great that couples choose to divorce and live apart from each other. Even in those situations we believe that the covenanting dimension which permeated the relationship in the beginning should still endure so that each member of the couple continues to recognize and respect the other's worth, rights, and dignity, and refuses to perpetuate or inflict unnecessary pain in the redefined relationship.

As a person I cannot grow to my capacity as a faith person simply by willing it and relying on my own internal resources. I shape my life as a Christian as I do relational work with God and with persons around me. I need the help of my spouse. That most intimate person in my life needs my help, too. We must commit ourselves to mutual faith growth.

Commitment to Faith Nurturing in Parenting

Writers of the Old Testament spoke of God's relationship with Israel in parent-child terms. The Lord is referred to as the Father (i.e. Isaiah 63:16, 64:8). The Lord is likened to a mother eagle with her young (i.e. Psalm 17:8, Deuteronomy 32:10-12). Time after time the people were asked to be faithful to the covenant with the living God, who had created them and given them life. They were told that even though they turned from God's ways and wandered into unfaithful living, God's love for them endured. They could return, and God would receive them. God's love as a parent was forever.

God informed the people how they should live within the covenantal relationship in many ways through outstanding leaders, in the law, the rituals of worship, the oral tradition of earlier faith pilgrims, and the traditions of family and clan. It seems as if the people should have known what covenantal living required of them, but they consistently chose other paths which seemed more appealing.

Jesus became God's living disclosure of trust and obedience. His life reflected covenantal faithfulness in every way. In him there was a clear portrayal of being faithful as a child of God. He showed us what it meant to do justice, to love steadfastly, and to walk humbly with God (Micah 6:8, paraphrased).

Insights from the Old and the New Testaments provide a guide for parents to realize the crucial task of committing themselves to nurturing their children in all of life. In particular, faith nurturing is a central parenting task, for it is through this process that children make the choices of what makes life meaningful and what kind of faith persons they will be.

It is interesting that faith nurturing of children happens whether parents are intentional or not. Professor James Fowler has confirmed that humans are faithful beings.[5] All of us make choices about the meaning of our existence. The question is not ''Will this person have faith?'' but rather ''What kind of faith will this person have? How will it be shaped? What will be its content? How consistent will it be?'' Children begin to learn about the nature of faith by imitating their parents. They soon learn what significant adults hold to be important. Power, money, entertainment, television, extended family, friends, church, the daily paper, boating, camping, the telephone, and eating are some entries for this potentially endless list. Children learn these crucial lessons even when parents have no intention of teaching them.

Some examples might help illuminate the outcomes of this kind of learning.

''Monday night is when Dad has his friends over to watch football.''

''We go camping in a tent, not a trailer.''

''We go to Gramma's every Saturday for dinner.''

''We don't spend Mom's and Dad's money for arcade video games.''

''We all have to drink diet soda when we go out for pizza because we buy it by the whole pitcher.''

''Every week someone has to dust the Bible on the coffee table, but no one ever reads it.''

Rarely are these kinds of things talked about, but every family members knows they are important. We all have a feel for where our time, energy, and sometimes financial resources go; but we may have no idea why. It just happens that way in our particular family.

If as parents we are serious about guiding children in their faith walk, then we need to examine what we are teaching children by the way we live. We must choose to live in certain ways because we want our children to grow in being faith persons as they imitate our ways of living.

In chapter 1 we noted that one of the responsibilities of Old Testament families was to raise children in the ways of the Lord. Through this process children became part of the faith community. When the time was right, they would in turn teach their children. In this manner the faith was passed from one generation to another. It was not so much that parents made a dramatic, well-considered choice to do as God commanded. Rather, the process was expected of faithful members of the people of God and was incorporated into their patterns of life.

For most of us in today's society, more deliberate thought has to go into how children in our care will be nurtured in faith. In his books *Future Shock* and *The Third Wave,* Alvin Toffler has pointed out that we live in a world with multiple value systems. What has a high priority in one schema may be devalued in another.

Commitment to the faith nurturing of children as they grow from helpless infants to independent adults gains unusual significance in these pluralistic value environs. As faith nurturers Christian parents will need to clarify the deepest meaning of the Christian faith. Incorporating this meaning into their own ways of living to portray a kind of living picture will take deliberate thought. Assisting children in exploring the world of multivalues in which they exist will be an important part of the process. Helping them grow in their capacities to make wise choices is an integral dimension of faith nurturing. The task is complex. It will require long-term and unwavering commitment of time and energy.

Even with two parents in the home sharing the faith-nurturing task, the responsibility is still an imposing one. In the case of single-parent families where mother or father assumes the entire parenting role for given periods of time, the responsibility is even more momentous. A recent issue of *Newsweek* magazine pointed out that in 1985 one out of four families in the United States is a single-parent household. By 1990 that figure could be one out of two.

We believe that in situations where it is at all possible both fathers and mothers should have input into the faith nurturing of their children. We recognize that this is not easy to implement. It implies that the divorced parents will have to investigate seriously the faith picture they are conveying through their treatment of each other. When the situation is such that one parent carries the entire load of raising the children, the decision about what faith nurturing in this family should look like may very well be easier because it now resides in one person. However, *accomplishing* the nurturing task may seem terribly imposing.

A surprise for many parents relating to their first child may be the realization that children have the mysterious ability to nurture parents in the faith. When our daughter, Mel, was four years old, she asked one question after another. Many of them were faith-oriented. Does God live in a big house? Where did God get ideas for making animals? Why did God let that bad car hit my kitty? In searching for appropriate responses—not necessarily answers—we found ourselves challenged to grow. Although they now are much more sophisticated in nature, Mel's questions still push us to investigate our own faith.

Tim's nurturing of us as parents has been a very different experience. Once when Jan was very ill, Tim, who was almost four, stood like a statue by her bed. When she opened her eyes, he smiled broadly and announced quietly but confidently, ''We prayed for you in Sunday school today. I told my teacher you were *very sick*! God will make you well, Mommy!'' He patted Jan's hand and left so ''Mommy could sleep!'' At a time when in our own faith we were struggling with doubts and uncertainty, Tim's simple faith statement renewed our hope. Getting well took weeks, months, and years. Along the way Tim in his own style helped us keep our faith alive and strong.

Being open to growth is an important element in committing oneself to nurturing children in the faith. Our children become the instruments for our own nurturance.

Extended families can be a rich resource for parents as they seek to implement ways of nurturing their children in the faith. Both of us remember the ways grandparents contributed to our faith growth.

One Christmas when Myron was a boy, his grandfather presented him with the complete Bible in comic-book style. Working his way through it again and again, Myron learned the Bible stories which have continued to inform him through his years of study, teaching, and preaching.

Grandmother Rhea lived with Jan's family until her death when Jan was almost five. Jan's memories of her grandmother are few and vague. One picture that does stand out is that morning ritual of Bible reading in one of the big leather rocking chairs in the farmhouse living room.

To be close to Grandmother during her Bible reading time meant to sit quietly by her side without saying one word. Obviously this kind of ritual was rigorous for a talkative preschooler. However, the experiences left deep impressions. Even today Jan expresses the feeling that something mysterious and wonderful had to have been happening for Grandmother to spend such a long time reading the extra-large, gold-trimmed, black Bible with hardly any pictures in it.

Fulfilling the commitment to nurture children in the faith is demanding. None of us as parents can be perfect in reaching our goal. God makes amazing use of earthen-vessel moms and dads. We are called to be faithful, not to be 100 percent effective.

We need to give ourselves some "grace" room. Many other persons in addition to parents affect a growing child. The entire task of nurturing faith in children, while central to parenting, does not belong to parents alone. It also belongs to the larger faith community. Reliance upon the leading and strengthening of the Holy Spirit as parents make decisions regarding faith nurturing will be sufficient for faithfulness to God's call. Commitments to nurture a marriage and to nurture children are central to family faith nurturing. It is also important to consider what commitments can be made to nurture the family as a whole.

The Family System's Commitment to Faith Nurturing

Given our conviction that Christian families are microcommunity churches, we are advocates that families must cultivate their identity as God's people.

Since some members of the family may not claim the Christian faith, the thrust to nurture the whole family will have to be adjusted to fit the situation. When either a husband or a wife does not espouse the faith, the task of determining how other family members who are Christians will live out their identity becomes a sensitive and sometimes difficult process. Hurdles may arise in the context of interfaith marriages in which wife and husband have not arrived at any workable agreement about how their faith differences will influence what actually happens in day-to-day family living.

Some families have never been challenged to consider the idea that their life together is a small but important expression of the church in the world. They may recognize the importance of nurturing individuals in faith growth but may not have considered the possibility of doing something as a total family group to enhance their understanding of what it means for their family to be the church in the world. They have never dreamed that concerted faith action on the part of the whole family is God's family at work.

As we pointed out in chapter 1, the mission of the church is to be shared by the family. One dimension of being the church is the attention given to the internal life of the people, in this case the family. Our ways of worshiping together, our bearing each other's burdens, our life of common prayer, our sharing of life's resources, our love for each other—all of these deserve our attention.

One family we know has worked very hard at being a family who prays together. When the children were small the family came together for times of corporate prayer. As the children grew to be teenagers and then young adults, the patterns of praying together changed to fit the new life stages. Although the members of this family now live at some distance from one another, they continue the discipline of common prayer concerns communicated to one another by phone or by letter.

Myron's family attended church activities together on a regular basis. Their picture of what it meant to be part of that family included being a church-going family.

One of our colleagues tells how her family regularly gathered while her father read from the Bible and from substantive theological works like Calvin's *Institutes*. While such a practice undoubtedly weighed heavy for restless children on many occasions, it had an effect on who those children became. They experienced their father's love for Scripture and theology. Today our colleague is a theologian continually working on both theological content and method. She attributes her early love for theology to the family practice of daily study.

One of the families in Jan's childhood church concentrated on giving loving support and upbuilding one another. It was a large family, and the father died leaving the mother to raise the children by herself. She insisted the only way they could survive as a family was by supporting one another. They did. Most of them eventually completed a college education; some received master's degrees. Some worked to pay expenses for others. When that stage was over for one person, the roles switched. When one brother was seriously injured in an accident and faced a long period of therapy and recuperation, one by one his sisters and brothers came home to help with his care. Each summer they all came home for a weekend to visit "Mom" and to be with one another. This family was known in the church and in the community as a family who knew how to love one another.

A second dimension of being the church as a family involves the external mission to those outside of the family or church. Jesus taught that the Good News should be taken to the ends of the earth. His ministry of preaching to the poor, proclaiming liberty to the captives, healing the blind and sick, and setting the oppressed free belongs to us now. Wherever there is unrest, war, or injustice, Christians are to be there to be light, salt, and leaven.

Just as each family has to shape its internal ministry, each family also shapes the ways in which it will bring the Good News to a hurting world. One family chose to "adopt" several students from Third-World countries so that they could obtain college educations. They have invested a decade in their ministry. Their outreach is extended until those young people complete their educations and return to their own countries to contribute to life there.

Another family has been involved in taking meals into the homes of the elderly. A related ministry is carried on by a family who visits nursing homes on a regular basis as clowns.

A number of families from an Episcopal parish joined together to help rebuild abandoned houses. These homes were purchased at very low prices and thereby became available to minority families with limited resources for making down payments and meeting high monthly mortgage bills.

Being the church as a family can take many forms. Each family needs to decide what best fits in its particular setting.

Mutual Commitment by Church and by Families

Faith nurturing in the context of marriages, parenting, and the entire family is a challenge requiring the investment of many resources. The family needs the help and support of the church. It is in the context of the church that families participate in worship and partake of the Lord's Supper together. Such participation is important to the formation of Christian identity.

Some churches have so many scheduled activities that they seem to do more to drain the time and energy resources of families than to build them up. It often seems as though churches assume that faith nurturing in the family will happen automatically. The ministry of the church simply involves regular worship, crisis ministry, and life passages such as baptism, marriage, and funerals. No special attention is given beyond these normal programs.

A growing number of congregations and their pastors are expressing concern about the need for specialized family ministries to families in their congregations. Christian families need a theology to help them define what Christian family togetherness means. Theories and skills to build more wholesome relationships and communication structures can be vital factors in strengthening the quality of shared living among Christians. A variety of resources made available for families to use in fostering both individual and family faith growth can be of tremendous value. Opportunities offered by the church for family mission to the world provide a link which might otherwise be inaccessible to families.

The commitment for help and support requires a mutual investment by both churches and families. There is no question that families stand in need of the church's ministry. Just as families need resources provided by the church in their task of faith nurturing, so healthy churches need full and enthusiastic participation by families that make up their membership. Family sociologist Dennis Guernsey observes that the best relationship between church and family is a symbiotic one.[7] Theologian J. Deotis Roberts makes a similar point.[8] The church and the family need each other, for they give life to each other.

It is not easy for families to commit themselves to participation in the life of God's people. Fathers work; mothers work. Their schedules hardly allow time to accomplish the necessities of keeping a home together. Children are in day care or school five days a week. There are dance classes, piano lessons, sports leagues, and scouting events. Teenagers have homework, school activities, projects, jobs, and "special friends." Television viewing consumes an incredible number of hours each day. In the midst of all the demands it becomes difficult to know how to make meaningful commitments to church life. Some families have found it easier to contribute money instead of time or presence. Church attendance becomes occasional; the family goes when it can squeeze it into the schedule. Families who move into this kind of pattern lose touch with the life of the church. The congregation as a whole loses touch with them.

If churches are to be strong and capable of providing resources to enhance faith nurturing, they must have the involvement and support of the families who comprise their membership. Mutual commitment is a necessity. The church and its families need each other.

If faith nurturing in the family is to happen in qualitative ways, persons must intentionally commit themselves to faith growth in themselves and in other family members. God's trustworthy and abiding covenantal love is the foundation from which Christian commitment to faith takes shape.

Questions for Reflection and Discussion

1. What ideas would you like to add to the theological core statement presented in this chapter?

2. What do you think about distinguishing between a wedding and a marriage? Is it a helpful distinction? Is it important?

3. In what ways do you agree that "relationships are hard work"? Do you have evidence from your own life?

4. Do you have illustrations from your life in which children have nurtured you in the faith?

5. To what extent do you agree with the authors' viewpoint that the church and families need each other?

PART TWO
Establishing a Climate for
Faith Nurturing in the Family

3

God's Love—A Model
for Faith Nurturing

Faith nurturing is vital to the well-being of the family and the faith community. Our commitment to the task is important. These were the primary points elaborated upon in Part 1. Now we might ask, "What is faith nurturing anyway? What are we trying to accomplish? How do we get started?

These are important questions. Researchers have raised them; individuals in our classes have asked them; we have faced them ourselves. In Part 2 we want to respond to these questions by exploring how using the model of God's love in our family living in trustworthy ways helps us establish a climate in which families can nurture faith.

In this chapter it is our task to identify and spell out seven dimensions of the love of the triune God. In chapter 4 we show how the love of the triune God applies to family living and to establishing a climate for nurturing faith. Chapter 5 points out the significance of developing trustworthy relationships as a context where faith can be nurtured. Through these three chapters our intent is to lift up the importance of establishing loving, trustworthy relational environments as basic to nurturing faith in families.

Authentic Caring—the Ground of Faith

Invariably, faith is rooted and nurtured through caring relationships that have the mark of integrity. Gordon Jackson discovered this truth in his study of 210 persons of faith. We have had his findings confirmed in our discussions with our students over the years.[1]

Authentic, trustworthy caring is what love is all about. Love is the

39

practice of active goodwill toward others. A more narrow definition for the purposes of this book might go like this: *love is the willful ability to entrust oneself to nurturing growth in another.*

Faith takes root and is nurtured within the context of loving and trustworthy relationships. This context is most likely to be present within the family and demonstrates why loving families are so fundamental to the formation of faith in persons.

The Triune God—the Source of Love

The beginning point for understanding such love is God, for the Creator/Redeemer God is the source of all genuine love. Indeed, the primary truth about God is that God is love.

This truth is shared by the whole Godhead. Each person within the Trinity exists in light of the other and for the other. Indeed, the Persons within the Trinity fulfill themselves in one another by virtue of self-surrendering love. Each Person, whether it be God the Creator, God the Son, or God the Spirit receives the fullness of eternal life from the love of the other members of the Trinity. The unity of the trinitarian Persons lies in their fellowship of eternal love. Each Person within the Trinity is nurtured by the love of the others. Each is brought into perfect form and beauty through the love of one another.

The Trinity as Family

If we are to understand these theological abstractions, it might be helpful to view the Trinity as corresponding to a human community without privileges and domination. The three divine Persons share everything in common, except for what makes each unique within the Godhead. So the Trinity is like a community of people who are defined through their relations with one another and in their unique importance to one another. Most importantly they are not in opposition to one another in terms of power and possession.

Some theologians use the image of family to express the unity of the Trinity: three Persons—one family. What this concept means is that people, not just individual persons, are made in the divine image. The image of God is person-with-person: Adam and Eve—or, as Gregory of Nazianzus, a fourth-century church father, put it, Adam and Eve and Seth, are an earthly image, a parable of the Trinity.[2]

The doctrine of the Trinity can be related to the family since both can be perceived as social systems in which persons relate and live. Love is basic to the life of both systems. Family members stand in caring relationship to one another in a way analogous to the way the members of the Trinity relate to one another. The human family has as its theological starting place the triune God. The Trinity of love provides the basis for the Christian family to be a community of love.

Jesus Christ—the Channel of God's Love

How can the love that exists within the Trinitarian Family inform our love for one another as family members? The key to understanding God's love is Jesus Christ; for he is the visible image of the invisible God (Colossians 1:15). God's love reaches humanity through Jesus Christ (John 17:22-26). We agree with Martin Luther, the great reformer, that in the embodiment of God in Christ, in the lowly life of the Word made flesh, in the suffering and death on the cross we have the clearest revelation of God that is possible for humans to have on this earth. This revelation clearly reveals the triune God's unconditional, active goodwill toward all of humanity. Indeed, Jesus Christ is the primary channel of God's communication of limitless love for human beings.

By being related to this God through Jesus Christ we place ourselves in one of the most personal of all possible relationships. According to the theologian Abelard, who lived about a thousand years ago, Jesus died on the cross to show us the love of God and to arouse within us a responding love. He died to reveal to us God's love so that we might in turn love others. The model of divine love as revealed in Jesus Christ becomes the model and the pattern for our living together as Christian families.

What then are some of the characteristics of the triune God's infinite love as revealed through Jesus? We examine only some, for the love of God is too big and too deep for human minds to comprehend fully or for authors like us to embody within the limitation of words. However, from our study of the life and teachings of Jesus within the context of the whole Bible, we have identified seven mutually interdependent dimensions of God's love for humanity.

Seven Dimensions of God's Love

Caring

The apostle Peter summed up the heart of the gospel of Jesus Christ in simple words: ''he cares for you'' (1 Peter 5:7). In the midst of life's sufferings and difficulties the word of revelation is that God is concerned about us. A God who cares is the particular treasure of Judaic and

Christian faith. At its highest development, Greek philosophy could form a doctrine of the perfect goodness of God, but it could not imagine in the divine an active concern for humanity.

A basic biblical image that conveys the caring nature of the triune God is the image of the shepherd caring for his sheep. The image of the people of God under a divine Shepherd is rooted deeply in the religious tradition of Israel. God was Israel's shepherd.

> The Lord is my shepherd,
> I shall not want. . . .
> > (Psalm 23:1, RSV)
> Give ear, O Shepherd of Israel,
> Thou who leadest Joseph like a flock! . . .
> > (Psalm 80:1, RSV)
> He will feed his flock like a shepherd,
> he will gather the lambs in his arms,
> he will carry them in his bosom,
> and gently lead those that are with young.
> > (Isaiah 40:11, RSV)

Israel was God's flock.

> And they shall know that I, the LORD their God, am with them, and that they, the house of Israel, are my people, says the Lord GOD. And you are my sheep, the sheep of my pasture, and I am your God, says the Lord GOD.   (Ezekiel 34:30-31, RSV)

The image of God as shepherd portrays the holy One as a strong, caring leader, for the shepherd is a strong man who is capable of defending his flock against wild beasts. He is also gentle with his sheep, and aware of their condition. He adapts to their needs, bears them in his powerful arms, and cherishes each and every one of them as his own child. The good shepherd is known for his faithfulness in finding grazing pastures and good watering-places, even in the midst of dark and cloudy weather. The shepherd has a concern for the well-being of the sheep that the hired hands lack. For example, the good shepherd will search for the one lost sheep and will lay down his life, if necessary, to save it. As God's people we find ourselves safe in the care of Jesus, the Good Shepherd.

God cared enough to send the Son. Indeed, Jesus understood himself to be the Good Shepherd who lays down his life for the sheep (John 10:11). Through faith in him we experience the life of God now and forever rather than alienation from God in the present and isolation beyond the grave. In the words of Henri J. M. Nouwen, a noted Catholic teacher and writer,

> the great mystery of our salvation is that God came to us in Jesus Christ, not first of all to take our pains away but to share them. He did not cling to his power to cure but cared. He cried out with us by entering so deeply in our human situation that nothing human is alien to him.[3]

This caring nature of God is most solidly revealed in the death and resurrection of our Lord. The old rugged cross both demonstrates and shows the measure of God's caring. God's love is caring.

Responsive

God's love is responsive to human need. The Eternal is something other than impersonal, creative energy behind and within the structures and processes of the universe. The Creator is something other than the Great Clockmaker, who created the worlds and now resides in some remote part of the cosmos. Indeed, the God of the Bible is a living God (Judges 8:19, 1 Kings 17:1). This Maker of heaven and earth is an extraordinarily active presence working to redeem the world. This Source of all life is intensely personal, for God emotes anger as well as tenderness.

But how is this divine Being responsive to people's needs? What is the nature of God's response?

Some, influenced by the fertility cults of the ancient Near East, pictured God as giving his or her followers whatever they craved. On the other hand, some within Israel saw God being responsive by rewarding and punishing individuals mathematically according to the morality of their actions. This view is characteristic of some of the historical material found in First and Second Chronicles. Both of these outlooks fail to allow for the personal as well as purposeful and voluntary character of God's faithful response to humanity.

God's responsiveness toward human need is marked by grace. Rather than abandoning humankind to the consequences of sin, God responds with acts of grace, the unmerited mercy of God toward humanity (Titus 3:3-7).

The Old Testament is filled with stories of a gracious God. After the flood God made a covenant with Noah promising never again to send a worldwide flood to judge humanity (Genesis 9:8-17). God called Abraham to found a people who would become a blessing to humankind. Rather than abandon humanity to its sinful consequences, God initiated a solution through Abraham (Genesis 12:2-3). God filled the womb of the elderly Sarah so that the family of the covenant made with Abraham could be a blessing to the nations through Isaac (Genesis 18:9-15, 21:1-7). In the Old Testament the most dramatic form of the grace of God comes in God's rescue of Israel from Egypt and the resulting covenant that God made with the nation at Mount Sinai (Exodus, chapters 1-34).

Through the death and resurrection of Jesus Christ we have received God's grace par excellence (John 1:17). Out of the depth of the holy One's caring love for lost humanity, God responded by sending us a child in Bethlehem (John 3:16). In Jesus Christ we behold the wonder of the triune God's grace (John 1:14) and discover that ''God is love'' (1 John 4:8).

God not only cares about human need, but also acts and responds to our need by relating us to the purposes of eternity. Since God is first, the Source of everything, there is no outside force coercing God to be responsible for the creation. God's love is an act of grace that grows out of the depths of divine compassion for weak, rebellious creatures. God's love is responsive.

Accountable

God's love is caring and responsive, but it is also accountable. Divine love is no insipid concern that operates without regard to the best interests of the humanity God loves. ''I will be your God, and you will be my people'' (Leviticus 26:12, Jeremiah 7:23) is at the heart and core of God's covenant with humanity. God has taken initiative toward humanity, first through Israel and then through the church, by responding with a gracious ''yes'' to our need for salvation. ''I will be your God'' means that God is related to humanity through covenant. God initiates the covenant and intends to be faithful to humanity.

''You will be my people'' means that the covenant cannot work without human beings responding to God's initiative. Humans are God's covenant partners and are accountable to God for keeping the law and ministering to the world. Human existence occurs within the context of ordered, accountable relationships that have ethical and moral implications. God calls humanity into relationship to the Holy. This God intends to be a faithful, trustworthy partner and requires the same qualities of the ones loved. However, Israel's history is a series of unfaithful acts by God's covenant people.

The metaphor of God as disciplinarian, derived from the parent-child relationship, is used by the Old Testament prophets to show how accountability works within the God-human relationship. Within this metaphor is the conviction that God loves the people of God and seeks their ultimate well-being; however, they must keep the divine commands as the necessary condition for human fulfillment. The children of God know that they are loved by the heavenly Father because this divine Parent exercises discipline upon them (Proverbs 3:11-12, Hebrews 12:5-8, Revelation 3:19). Such divine accountability is loving because it leads us to holiness and the righteous life (Hebrews 12:10-11).

Accountability in relationships was clearly embodied in the life of Jesus when he drove the traders out of the temple (Matthew 21:12-13). He also held his disciples accountable when they fell asleep while he was at prayer in the Garden of Gethsemane (Mark 14:32-42).

God is faithful and seeks faithfulness in the recipients of graceful love. This trustworthy God demands accountability in divine and human relationships. Such accountability is always motivated by divine love, for such love realizes that the blessings of life are accomplished through living responsibly within relationships. God can be counted on, for covenantal love is loyal and steadfast; such love is eternal (Psalm 136). Such eternal love is the profound mystery of the birth, life, death, resurrection, and ascension of our Lord Jesus Christ. God's love is accountable.

Giving

God revealed love for us by giving the most precious possession a parent can give, one's only child (John 3:16). In Christ God gave of that which is alive in the divine Being—love, joy, peace, patience, kindness, goodness, faithfulness, humility, and self-control—the fruit of the Spirit (Galatians 5:22-23). Through the divine life of Jesus Christ, God enriches us and enhances our sense of being alive. Such generosity toward sinners might be considered foolishness according to the ways of this world, but within the divine plan it is the power of God unto salvation (1 Corinthians 1:18).

However, God's generous love generates in us the quality of life that makes us really alive as responsible human beings. The love of God awakens in us the faith by which we are absolutely dependent upon God. Through our trust in God the Holy Spirit sets humanity free for the highest form of human activity—love.

In the act of God's gift of grace in Jesus Christ a relationship of mutual love is born. The power of God's generous love has made it possible for us to become the Lord's children—the children of love

(John 1:12, 1 John 3:1-2).

The power of God's love in Jesus Christ can be measured through its capacity to generate love in those for whom it has been given. God's gift of love liberates us from bondage to ourselves and to the world and sets us free to love God and neighbor. It is the only life resource that has a future in this age of death. God's love is giving.

Knowing

God, above all others, knows us through and through. Because the Creator cares for us, God seeks knowledge of us. God is not divinely curious nor does God seek knowledge of us for the sake of having power over us. God seeks to be in communion with us, for we are the Redeemer's covenant partners.

God's way of knowing us is quite different from our usual objective ways of knowing. We who live in the Western world have been greatly influenced by the Greek philosophers. From their perspective we "know" something only insofar as we are detached from it. We collect information about a person or object as it exists apart from or outside of ourselves. We contaminate or distort our knowledge by becoming emotionally involved with what we want to know.[4]

From the perspective of God revealed through Jesus Christ it is impossible to know anything about persons without being in relationship to them. God knows us because Christ came and lived in our midst (John 1:14). The Ruler of the universe knows us because this gracious God chose to become intensely involved with us by becoming one of us in Jesus Christ (Philippians 2:5-8). Jesus lived in such close relationship with us that he understands our most intimate sufferings and temptations (Hebrews 2:17-18, 4:15). His knowledge penetrates to the very core of our existence (Psalm 44:21; John 2:25, 10:14-15).

God's knowledge of us has several results. With such knowledge of us Jesus Christ makes possible our being reconciled to God by being the expiation for our sins (Hebrews 2:17-18). Because God's knowledge of us is a relational knowledge, we are invited to be in dialogue with this ever-loving God. The channel for such dialogical communion is prayer. As God's dialogue partners, we are able to become our covenant Partner's friend (John 15:15, James 4:4). Such friendship with God places us in a relationship of intimate affection with the Creator. God's knowledge of humanity guides divine love. To know us so intimately is to know our every need and to see the paradoxical nature of human beauty and depravity. Without the knowing dimension of love God's caring, responsiveness, and giving toward us could lead to sentimentality and blindness regarding our true nature. The accountable dimension of divine love could become either harsh and unjust or permissive.

Because of God's knowledge of us through Jesus, we experience a love that meets our deepest human need: life in relationship with the triune God. God's love is knowing.

Respectful

A love which is caring, responsive, accountable, giving, and knowing could easily degenerate into domination and possessiveness were it not for the dimension of respect. Rather than referring to fear and awe, respect in the context of divine love considers people worthy of esteem because of their unique individuality. Respect makes room for other persons to grow and develop as God has created them.

In genuine love the distinction between oneself and another is always kept. Respectful love perceives the object of love as someone who has a completely separate identity. Respect implies the absence of exploitation; indeed, it exists on the basis of freedom. An old French song states, "love is the child of freedom, never that of domination."[5]

Such an understanding of what it means to respect grows out of how God has approached us in Jesus Christ. The holy One's approach to us is through the manger of Bethlehem and the cross of Calvary rather than through the coercive power of some celestial SWAT team. In leaving to us the choice to believe in him (John 3:16, 36), God respects our individuality and freedom. God has created us to be free and worthy, for God has created us in the divine image (Genesis 1:27, 9:6).

In seeking to redeem us God does not deny what has been affirmed in creation; rather, the eternal Presence respects our right to choose with integrity this caring, responsive, and giving love of God. God is Creator, and humans are creatures. This distance between Creator and creature makes possible our freedom, our volition, and our growth. God has a deep respect for the otherness of humanity and a profound willingness to respect our integrity. When we respond in faith to the love of God as revealed in the Son, our individuality, worth, and freedom are confirmed in our union with Christ. God respects our freedom to accept or reject divine love.

An example from the life of Jesus illustrates this truth about God's love. One day a man ran up to Jesus and knelt before him and asked, "Good teacher, what must I do to receive eternal life?"

"Why do you call me good? No one is really good except God. You know the commandments: 'Do not commit adultery; do not steal; do not accuse anyone falsely; do not cheat; honor your father and your mother,'" Jesus responded.

"Teacher," the man stated, "since I was very young, I have obeyed all these commands."

Jesus looked him straight in the eyes with caring love and said, "You need to do only one thing then. Go, sell all your possessions and give the money to the poor, and then you will have riches in heaven. After that come and follow me."

When the man heard the choice that he had to make, gloom spread over his face. He went away very sad, because he was very rich and could not say yes to Jesus' way to eternal life (paraphrase of Mark 10:17-22).

Jesus cared about this rich man, but he did not force him into the kingdom of God. He confronted the rich man with his spiritual poverty but respected his choice to stay with his riches rather than pay the cost of discipleship and follow Jesus. Because of his warm, caring love Jesus drew near to the rich man but did not force him, exploit him, dominate him, manipulate him, or absorb him—for God's love is respecting.

Forgiving

For God in Christ to know us in our weakness (Hebrews 4:15), our blindness (Luke 19:41-42), and our disloyalty (Luke 22:48) could lead to our judgment and condemnation. However, God's knowledge of us in Jesus Christ leads to forgiveness rather than condemnation. This caring creator God, who values the wayward creature, sent the Son into the world to be its Savior rather than its Judge (John 3:17).

The story of the waiting father in Luke 15:11-32 beautifully articulates the uncondemning nature of God. The younger son demanded his inheritance before it was due. He took it, left home, and squandered it. Realizing what he had done, he returned home with no more demands. He wanted only to have the status of a hired worker. Because of his compassion, however, the father received him with joy and returned to him the full status of sonship. This is a beautiful parable of the forgiving love of God.

However, one essential element is missing from the story: the cost of forgiveness. The compassionate One's forgiving love rests basically on the Savior's suffering upon the cross. In the parable of the prodigal, the love of the waiting father could be seen as the permissive sentiment of an unjust parent. The older brother saw his father in this way. However, God's love lacks sentimentality, for the power of God's love is energized and realized by the Suffering Servant's giving his life's blood upon the cross (Ephesians 1:7, Matthew 26:28). The suffering of Calvary reveals the depth of God's forgiving love and the seriousness of the divine purpose to save humanity.

No power has been greater in breaking through the human condition than this act of suffering, forgiving love. God's love, which has come into our world through the manger and the cross, is a pardoning love. Jesus brings forgiveness of sins. When we experience forgiving love, a completely new power of overflowing love is released within us. History is filled with persons whose lives have been transformed by the power of God's forgiving love. People like the apostle Paul, Augustine, Martin Luther, and many others have known such forgiving love. By receiving Jesus' forgiveness of sins we know ourselves to be loved and freed from self-bondage for love. Our love for others is rooted in the depths of God's forgiving love (Luke 7:47). Indeed, God's forgiving love forms the foundation for a new relationship among human beings.

God's love was so deep that the Lord God gave and forgave that we might share in eternal life now and forever (John 3:16). The power of the bloodstained cross lies in the suffering, forgiving love of God as revealed through Jesus Christ. God's love is forgiving.

Responding to God's Love

Caring, responsive, accountable, giving, knowing, respectful, and forgiving—these seven mutually interdependent dimensions of love draw some of the lines upon the parental face of the triune God whom we know and experience as love through Jesus Christ. These same dimensions need to be recognized in family members and in family relationships.

Indeed, God's love seeks a response from its receivers. Divine love calls into being a community of love which is summoned into responsible action.[6] For the Christian family the formation of a community of love begins in the home. One of the family's most important tasks is nurturing its members in faith, hope, and love. As a community of love the Christian family exists from God and for God; it does not live for itself alone. The Christian family, like the larger community of faith, is the creation of God's forgiving love, but at the same time it is called to be an instrument or channel of divine love. The Christian family's very life is to be one of love; it is to embody love's power and work in society.

How this model of God's love is related to establishing a climate for faith nurturing in the family is the subject of our next chapter.

Questions for Reflection and Discussion

1. What experiences in your life confirm that faith takes root and is nurtured within the context of loving relationships?

2. If someone asked you to describe God, what would you say, given that Jesus is "the visible likeness of the invisible God" (Colossians 1:15)?

3. Are all of the seven dimensions of God's love—caring, responsive, accountable, giving, knowing, respectful, and forgiving—equally important? On what did you base your response?

4. Are there other dimensions of God's love which you think are important and have not been covered by those that have been identified and discussed? What are they? Why are they important?

5. Is God's love full and complete even if persons do not respond? What is your thinking?

4

Nurturing Love
in the Family

The love of the triune God provides a starting place for the family to be a community of love. Christian families must commit themselves to establishing a climate for nurturing deep and authentic human love among their members. Their love becomes a parable, a sign, of God's love. The ways in which they live point to the ways in which God has been faithful in relationship with humanity. The seven dimensions of God's love can serve as models for shaping relationships among the members of Christian families. For purposes of applying the dimensions of God's love to qualitative family living, we have identified the following relational love factors: care and responsiveness, accountability, giving and receiving, knowing and respecting, and finally, forgiving. To the extent that these love factors are present in the family, a climate for optimal faith growth will be created.

The human love factors we have identified are of basic importance, but they are not necessarily exhaustive. You may identify other factors. We would invite you to add your own factors to our list for reflection and implementation in your family living.

The love factors are not presented in strict sequential order. While we do see caring and responsiveness as basic, all are interdependent on one another. Any change in one affects the others.

Care and Responsiveness

The first love factors are based on the central affirmation that God cares for us. God's love is not impersonal, passive caring. Because God cares for us, God responded to humanity's condition through the grace gift of Jesus, the only Son. In our families we are to care for and respond to each other.

Responsiveness is the action component of caring. Without a fitting response, there is no certainty that the caring love is genuine. The quality of response serves as an indicator of the presence, depth, and duration of care.

A father was deeply hurt when his first child died of a serious illness. He vowed to himself and to God that he would never be vulnerable to that kind of pain and hurt again. He deliberately decided that when other children were born into the family he would provide a beautiful home and more than adequate material provisions for them. However, he absolutely refused to become deeply involved with them as persons. He believed he could not endure the pain if another of his children died. One by one his children grew into adolescence and then adulthood wondering if their father really cared. They could affirm his ability to provide, but they questioned his capacity to care.

Just as God's love shown in Jesus Christ became a picture for us to see God's loving response to us, so our own actions create pictures for others. These living pictures make our love believable or create an image of shallow, hollow words that speak of love but do not show it! Care which is made concrete in action creates a picture of genuine, enduring love.

Care and Responsiveness in Marriage

Empirical studies on long-term marriages have shown that in the context of enduring relationships each person feels valued and cared for by the other.[1] One judgment that divorced persons frequently make on their previous marriage goes something like this: "My spouse didn't care. I didn't care. We just quit caring. There's no point in going on if you don't care."

Evelyn and Paul Moschetta have researched marriages that possessed an unusual quality of intimacy. This intimacy resulted in each partner's being strongly independent yet strongly connected intellectually, emotionally, sexually, and spiritually.[2] They found three specific characteristics of these couples. All are aspects of caring.

In *sustenance caring* each person supplies the other with life's emotional necessities. In *intentional caring* persons deliberately become involved in assisting each other's growth toward full potential. Finally, in *reverential caring* each partner feels fully known, profoundly valued, and deeply loved by the other. From their discussions, it is obvious that for the Moschettas caring includes appropriate responsiveness on the part of each spouse for the other.

The Moschettas also observed that caring for each other seemed to come easily for some couples. These couples are the "naturals." Somehow these persons had inner resources from which to draw in order to be caring mates to each other. Most of these persons came from healthy, happy homes where they had felt loved and valued by their parents.

The Moschettas also discovered that other couples found the road to marital caring and appropriate responsiveness much more difficult. Caring did not come naturally or easily for them. They had to grow to become caring mates. It is encouraging to note that such growth does happen. Couples can improve the quality of caring between them.

There is much to learn about caring and responding to each other. As time passes the nature of a marriage relationship changes. The way each person responds to the other needs to adjust to the relational changes.

What one person perceives to be caring may be seen as quite the opposite by the other. A husband may take care of all financial matters which he believes is a way to communicate to his wife, "I know all of these details are a hassle. I love you. I will take care of them so you won't have to worry. I will protect you from the stress." As time goes by the wife sees the husband's response as one of control and power rather than love and care. From her viewpoint he has succeeded in keeping her helpless and dependent. She has no awareness of how to handle financial matters. She develops the conviction that if her husband really cared for her, he would teach her.

All kinds of life arenas can become the focus of these "I-care-for-you!"/"No,-you-don't" tensions between husbands and wives who see things very differently. If these tensions are discussed openly and feelings are shared, adjustments can be made to negotiate both more accurate interpretations and more appropriate responses.

Marital caring and responsiveness must be nurtured as the years of marriage go by. Husbands and wives need each other to facilitate this process, which for most couples may not be easy or natural. For all couples these love factors require attention, so that caring and responsiveness deepen and become more abiding. It is in the context of deep marital caring that individuals are free to pursue their life potential, that the relationship flourishes, and that faith finds an optimal growth climate. Quality caring and appropriate responsiveness are foundational if a relationship is to endure.

Care and Responsiveness in Parenting

Parental caring and responsiveness begin early in life. Mothers are "bonded" to their newborn infants in the early minutes of life. Today many fathers are present in the delivery room to assist their wives, to witness the birth, to hear the sounds of the first breath, and to hold the baby in their arms. This initial bonding is important in parent/child love.

This summer our daughter brought a four-month-old girl from Korea to her adoptive family in the United States. Before the plane arrived, her new parents and her brother had only seen pictures of her. When the baby finally reached them, they experienced a whole new reality. The baby was "home." There were hugs, kisses, and admiring stares. Immediately they began to repeat her name over and over again. The seven-year-old brother stood tall and announced proudly, "That's my sister!" Within two minutes he repeated the announcement as if he had never said it before, "That's my *new* sister!" Even though they had held her for only a few minutes, there was no question that this family cared for its newest member. They cared not because this particular baby had contributed in great and significant ways to their well-being. They cared because she was a part of their family. Those of us who were witnesses to this unique and precious event were touched. Tears fell as we watched this event unfold.

The emotional glow of early bonding provides a resource base that parents draw from as they walk through sleepless nights, strive to determine the reason behind the high-pitched scream, and clean up one mess after another. The parenting walk is a long one filled with joys and complicated by a myriad of tasks.

For most parents, caring for and responding to children brings a number of rewards. Children themselves respond to their parents with happy smiles, bright eyes, and contagious giggles. "Thanks, Dad" or "I love you, Mom."

During some periods, however, caring and responding can be much more difficult and draining. The demands of being a parent seem overwhelming. Ambiguities cloud the path ahead. Parents experiencing these uncertain times may wonder if their caring is deep enough to sustain them from one day to the next.

Caring and responding must be cultivated and shaped as life moves along. Questions of one kind or another have to be confronted by parents. Some that we have faced or that others have shared with us may help you clarify your own set of questions.

Does caring always express itself in warm, tender feelings? Is caring tough and unyielding at points? How great is the risk when parents care deeply for their children? Can a parent care too much? Can a parent overrespond—to the detriment of the child? What is the result of failing to respond sufficiently or appropriately? Is it natural to care for and respond to each of your children differently? Is it natural not to care at all at times? Does caring always have to translate into action? Perhaps you recognize some questions you have dealt with or are facing.

While we have tried to identify and address our parenting questions as we have confronted them, we haven't always found adequate or satisfactory answers. Sometimes the answers were valid only for a limited period of time. As people and circumstances changed, we found ourselves searching for new and different answers.

One challenge in parental caring is guiding developing children to become persons with a capacity to care for and respond to others. Small children have a world view centered around the self. That is the world they know through experience. Helping them gradually move toward being sensitive, empathic individuals who care for others can be an involving, time consuming, and sometimes bewildering experience for parents. The ways in which the parent cares for and responds to the child become models for the child to imitate, but children often learn at a slower and less consistent pace than parents would like.

Establishing an environment in family living where deep caring and appropriate responding permeates the relationships is basic to creating a climate where faith nurturing can flourish.

Accountability

Being mutually accountable in relationships is essential if the persons involved are to be independent and emotionally healthy and if the relationship is to deepen and demonstrate integrity. God was the Covenant Giver, but humans as covenant receivers were asked to live in ways which led to holiness and righteous living. God required covenantal faithfulness from the Chosen People.

Personal histories in which relational accountability to each other has broken down are usually very sad. One wife tells how her abusive husband became increasingly violent. As years passed he moved from abusive shouting to physically beating her and then to beating the children. Finally, the parents separated and divorced, leaving that mother with five children, no regular child support, and a below-poverty-level income. The father moved to another state and never sees the children. Mutual accountability between that husband and wife had broken down very early in their marriage. "Right after we were married he began yelling at me all of the time. Then he started to hit me. I didn't say anything. I was afraid it would make him worse. I just lived with it. When he started hitting the kids and throwing them around, I thought I'd better do something. I wasn't sure what to do. It was my oldest daughter who finally told him to get out. I should have done it a long time ago. I just couldn't make myself do it."

Another story of broken accountability was shared by parents whose teenage daughter had left home. Days went by and she made no contact by phone or letter. Eventually, she called with the declaration, "I'm coming back to get my things—but I never want to see you two again." She returned for her things while her parents were away. The parents have not heard from her since. Through tears and choked voices they tried to spell out how much they cared for this daughter. "We loved her so much," they said. They gave several illustrations of their love; one stood out. "Even when she and her friends did several hundreds of dollars worth of damage to the house at one of their parties, we hardly said anything. We just had it all fixed up. We didn't think they realized what they were doing. Teenagers can get carried away."

Being accountable in qualitative relationships is essential and involves living responsibly with others. Achieving mutual accountability requires dedicated involvement on everyone's part. As persons grow in their accountability to one another, a trustworthy relational climate is formed where authentic faith can take root.

Accountability in Marriage

The question of accountability probably never occurs to the bride and groom as they come before the altar to exchange vows. For many couples, the assumption is that the love which unites them is so deep and so enduring that the issue of accountability will never come between them.

It often takes only a short time before the couple face the issue of being accountable to each other. They have arrived at understandings and commitments in their relationship. To what extent will they fulfill them? The issue may be raised over a seemingly trivial issue like whether the toilet seat is left raised or is returned to a horizontal position. We sometimes use this example at marriage enrichment retreats. Inevitably there are knowing glances, amused chuckles, or revealing nudges exchanged by a number of couples. They have dealt with this issue or others much like it. They recognize the territory. The know the questions.

Accountability involves living responsibly in relationship to each other. It encompasses a range of life issues from things like lowering toilet seats, putting caps on toothpaste or milk bottles, setting alarms, and unrolling dirty socks to consequential things like financial management, sexual fidelity, protection of self-worth, and reliability in following through on major agreements.

Accountability can be achieved if both husband and wife are involved mutually in the process. Issues have to be identified and discussed. Both persons have to express their perceptions and expectations. Standards and goals should be agreed upon by both partners. As the issues are confronted in daily living, husbands and wives need to give each other feedback as to how they are doing in meeting the standards.

Tensions often arise because some steps in the process have not been negotiated. For example, one person fails to meet the expectations of the other. These particular expectations have not been discussed. The one who feels disappointed and let down begins to keep score. An avalanche of anger breaks loose. The ''offender'' is shocked, having been totally unaware of having failed in some way.

Accountability functions best when issues are clear and standards have been negotiated fairly. If the standards are realistic and if they function to lead persons toward righteous living, they help to provide a structure and goals where husband and wife grow into a responsible Christian lifestyle.

Accountability in Parenting

We (Myron and Jan) believe that when a child is born or adopted into a family, parents have made a long-term stewardship commitment to nurturing that child toward autonomous adulthood. Such a commitment involves many things including meeting basic needs for physical safety, comfort, security, belonging, and affirmation. It includes being available to that child in a healthy relationship that is marked by love, fairness, and personal presence. Anyone who parents well has assumed a great deal of responsibility for a rather large segment of that child's life history.

When two persons are undertaking the parenting task together, they can walk the road side by side. They can discover ways to hold each other accountable to the parenting commitment. One can be strong when the other is burned out. One can say to the other, ''I believe you are doing one thing with the kids and I am doing another. We need to talk about it and get our act together,'' or ''I wonder if you are expecting too much from a four-year-old,'' or ''I'm so tired of fighting teenage battles in this house, I need your help,'' or ''You have spent so much time on the kids' projects; don't you think you need a break?''

Single parents face a different situation. There isn't another adult readily available to engage in parenting-accountability dialogue. It may be helpful to join a support group or ask friends or relatives to act as listeners and reactors in helping the single parent become accountable in parenting.

Holding another parent accountable is one thing; holding children accountable is something quite different. Many ambiguities surround the task. Questions raised are often difficult to answer with any precision.

To what extent are discipline and punishment the same? Could they be two entirely different things? At what age should children be held accountable for certain tasks and ways of relating? How does the parent take the uniqueness of the child into consideration? Should punishment be used only as a last resort?

You may be able to add your own questions to this partial list. We believe distinguishing between discipline and punishment is helpful. We see punishment as punitive action taken because someone has broken a rule or a law. The intent of punishment is to extinguish undesirable behavior. Discipline has to do with life control and living within boundaries and according to rules and standards that have been carefully defined as one's value system. The goal is that persons grow to be self-disciplined. Infants and small children have little self-control. They have many things to learn. They require a great deal of assistance from parents. As they grow and gain experience, they need the freedom to take control of their own behavior.

Holding children accountable is a complicated and awesome task. Perhaps parents err the most when they either oversimplify the process with too many easy answers or when they make the process so complicated that no one can follow it. In either case they are likely to end up abdicating any responsibility for holding children accountable.

As parents hold children accountable, they may discover that their children reciprocate. Rather than being offended and defensive, parents might well consider that such reciprocation is an indication that they are doing a good job with accountability issues in the family.

As the dialogical give and take of accountability occurs, the opportunity is there to assist each other in shaping a lifestyle that increasingly conforms to the faith standards of righteous living. By establishing a climate where accountability is taken seriously, we can grow in our capacity for Christian living. We will improve in our ability to interact responsibly with those around us.

Giving and Receiving

God's love is a giving love that is extended to us through the gift of Jesus. This divine love was given freely and without condition, and it models for us that our love must have a giving dimension as we reach out to other members of our family. We all have received God's love. Our love for one another must have a receiving dimension. As we approach each other, we have the need and the capacity to be both givers and receivers. The goal is to balance the two dynamics appropriately. If we constantly give and rarely receive, we deprive others of the joy of giving and run the risk of total depletion. If we receive and only give on rare occasions, we become a kind of relational parasite dependent on others' resources.

Jan's father knew how to give in many ways and on many levels. Rarely were his gifts controlling. Dad Duncan's love gifts were freely presented with few if any strings attached. He gave time and presence, money and gifts, and encouragement and advice from his own experience. He shared his personal talents, thoughts, and feelings. He gave to his wife, two daughters, extended family, friends, neighbors, and the community. He was known for his thoughtful, giving ways. In his life Jan saw reflected what it meant to give to others.

However, Dad Duncan kept a closed door when it came to receiving from others. He didn't accept help easily. Giving him satisfactory presents for Christmas or birthdays seemed impossible. There was no way to achieve a giving/receiving balance with him. It was only in the last few years of his life, when his mind was clouded and his body weak, that he was forced to receive help. Even then we could sense an underlying resentment. Given her family background, Jan has had to struggle to gain perspective on giving and receiving. The learning has taken years and continues even today.

Balancing giving and receiving becomes a goal for qualitative family relational living. Through the balance we experience the gift dimension of the Christian faith and thereby grow in our own capacity to give to and receive from others.

Giving in Marriage

Some persons talk about both husband and wife each giving 100 percent in a marriage. Others set the figure at 50 percent each. The point to be made is that both members of the marriage should be prepared to give their share to a marriage.

If each person is expected to give, then each person must be able to receive. In some marriages the flow of giving and receiving is smooth and deeply satisfying. For many others achieving any kind of satisfactory balance comes only through continual struggle.

To be satisfying, giving should relate to the needs of both persons. Giving is complementary if one person has a need to give something that matches what the other is ready and open to receive. For instance, a husband enjoys being told verbally by his wife that she loves and cares for him. This particular wife finds fulfillment when she voices these messages of affirmation several times a day.

However, giving becomes much more complex when the two needs are not so well synchronized. A wife grew up in a family where there was a great deal of touching to express love. She brought her need to give hugs and kisses to her husband whose family rarely touched in caring ways. He experiences her as a clinging vine. Initially this couple mutually frustrated each other. There were a number of ways to address and resolve the issue. This couple had to find their way.

Owning the mismatch problem, facing it, and shaping a mutually satisfactory solution will help couples learn to give and receive in rewarding ways. Ignoring or denying the tension is likely to lead to mounting irritation within both partners.

Achieving an appropriate balance of giving and receiving is an ongoing pilgrimage. The balance of giving and receiving has to be readjusted regularly to meet the needs generated by life's circumstances.

Illness, death of loved persons, financial crises, job pressures, and other stressful circumstances can introduce unevenness into the giving/receiving balance. As long as both persons are aware of the dynamics and willing to discuss the implications for their relationships, these periods may be difficult but not impossible. When couples refuse to admit that the unbalance exists or ignore the importance of negotiation or rebalancing, one or both persons can feel misunderstood and abused. These negative feelings complicate the process of regaining a more reasonable balance in better or more settled times.

Giving and receiving in mutually rewarding, balanced ways is fundamental to marital satisfaction. It also promotes growth toward becoming the persons God intends for us to be.

Giving in Parenting

The foundational gift parents give to children is that of life itself. Even in adopting children parents give the necessary love and attention to the dependent child that affirm that this life, although resulting from the union of others, will survive and receive nurture. The basic needs which the infant has are sleep, food, safety, elimination, and love. Parents sometimes feel that parenting is one-way giving. The process becomes more reciprocal over time. Parents experience moments of delightful receiving as the baby learns to squeeze a finger, focus attention on the parent's face, and smile spontaneously.

The giving of parents to their children lays the foundation for the child to grow toward becoming an adult who has the capacity for both giving and receiving in human relationships. If such healthy development is to happen, however, moms and dads must discover ways for their children to give in response to having received a great deal.

Children's gifts reflect their life stage. A nine-month-old will offer a reciprocal pat on the cheek. A two-year-old may suddenly thrust out a slobbery lollipop to share a lick with Mom. At six another child proudly answers the telephone so it will not disturb Dad as he's watching the news. At thirteen a teenager may remember to keep the radio at a ''reasonable decibel level.'' These gifts from children to their parents are a central part of learning to be giving persons in adulthood. A thoughtful response on the part of the parent helps children to experience the completed cycle.

Parents always face the dilemma of knowing where to draw lines on both giving and receiving. Because children in a family are different from one another, the lines drawn with one child may prove to be unhelpful or even destructive with another.

At age five our son, Tim, attended a six-week community-sponsored workshop on art for children. On the Saturday morning they finished ''sculpturing'' he presented us with a lopsided, murky-brown dinosaur. ''I made it 'specially for you,'' he told us. It sat on our bedroom dresser for an entire year. During summer cleaning, we moved the dinosaur to a drawer. The next day Tim inquired about the ''missing status'' of his creation. It obviously bothered him that we had put it away. We talked about it. Tim had deep feelings of mourning and pain. We decided to restore the dinosaur to its place on the dresser. This time it stayed there for several years. When he was nine, he seemed to feel ''okay'' about putting it away in the drawer. It is still there today and Tim is seventeen!

You probably can think of similar stories to tell from your own life. The stories help to illustrate the complexity of family giving and receiving. The dynamics often involved feelings of self-worth. These are rarely overtly stated, but they pervade what happens and how persons feel about the giving and receiving process.

Negotiating giving and receiving dynamics in family living creates a relational fabric where God's gift of the only Son can be affirmed and received at life-changing levels.

Knowing and Respecting

God's love for us is both knowing and respecting. God knows us more thoroughly than we know ourselves. God respects that which is known about us. God's love refuses to force or manipulate, but rather draws close waiting for our freely chosen response.

The love factors of knowing and respecting are vital in family living if we are to facilitate the growth of each person toward wholeness. Neither knowing nor respecting is easily achieved. Neither happens automatically.

Because family members share space, interact regularly with one another, and engage together in a large number of tasks, we would expect that family members would know one another better than anyone else. Yet many times, it appears as though "outsiders" know more about our family members than we do. Genuine knowing comes through qualitative relationships with one another. It is possible to be part of a family in which one feels like a stranger, feels misunderstood and misjudged. If one dimension of authentic love is expressed through relational knowing, then families may be confronted with the need to change their living patterns so they include this dimension of relating.

Another dynamic is added to love when one moves beyond knowing to respecting. A respecting person will not attempt to force, exploit, dominate, or absorb the other person. Rather, the other person is regarded as a separate person equally precious in God's sight.

Knowing and Respecting in Marriage

The marriage relationship holds great potential for knowing and being known by another human being in the deepest possible sense. When such knowing fails to happen, intense hurt and pain can result.

One husband living for a period in separation from his wife and children reflected on his situation. In evaluating his relationship with his wife he observed, ''I don't think we ever really knew each other. We probably got married for all of the wrong reasons. I even got to the point where I didn't like the stranger I was trying to live with. I had to get out.''

He continued to describe insights about his wife that he was gaining through some marital and family counseling in which both of them were participating. ''I had no idea she felt that way. She never told me! If she told me, I didn't hear it! She has said some things in that therapy room that really shocked me. If only I would have known her better, I. . . .'' He stopped before finishing the sentence.

Knowing another person in marriage is a mutual process whereby both persons grant each other permission to enter their inner worlds of thoughts and feelings. The process requires considerable time and commitment to in-depth sharing. As the extent of knowing increases so does vulnerability. The process will continue to be productive as long as each person remains confident that the other will responsibly and lovingly cherish the knowledge he or she possesses and use it to promote health and growth rather than to inflict pain. There is something sacramental about two persons entrusting deep knowledge of the self to each other.

Gaining knowledge of one's spouse is an ongoing process. Persons change a great deal with the passage of life. Every change presents a challenge to the spouse to continue ''knowing'' the other person.

As one's knowledge of the spouse increases, the need to exercise respect for the spouse also increases. With knowledge of the spouse's inner self the possibility of manipulation and domination increases. The power of enduring love at this point is respecting the sacredness of the spouse and leaving that person free to choose, grow, and become in ways appropriate to who he or she is.

One of the most sensitive areas of marital life in which knowing and respecting is required is sexual union. Through intercourse each ''knows'' the other in a depth not possible any other way. Each one is able to fulfill the other's needs because he or she respectfully brings to the sexual union deep knowledge of the other. Relational ecstasy happens!

Without knowledge and respect sexual intercourse can lead to feelings of having been dominated, used, or thwarted. Over time the sexual arena can become a relational battleground where power moves and counterpower responses predominate. As a result a negative legacy of personal hurts continues to accumulate.

All areas of marital living become more rewarding when couples are committed to implementing love factors which place a priority on mutual knowledge and respect. Knowing and respecting contribute to the wholesomeness of the climate in which faith nurturing can take place.

Knowing and Respecting in Parenting

When a baby enters a family, it doesn't take long for everyone else to realize that a unique personality with likes and dislikes has joined the family system. Our infant son detested being fed vegetables and would spew them out of his mouth. As regularly as we tried to introduce them into his diet, he would signal his distaste. It paid to know and to respect his preference if we wanted to avoid the attack!

If parents are to engage in effective nurturing of their children, it is essential that they know and respect the individuality of each child. Parenting methods and approaches which bring positive results with one child may be ineffective or may even produce negative results with another child. One child may require more direct and overt punishment than another child. Children differ in interests and abilities. If parents are to cultivate ways to develop each child's strongest points and interests, they must first know who that child is.

Sometimes parents have only superficial knowledge and minimal respect for the individuality of a child because they attempt to fulfill their own dreams through the child. Even though the child resists overtly, the parent may continue to push the child into one activity after another.

One middle-aged man described himself as having been an absolute failure to himself and to his family. At forty he was still trying to hold a steady job for more than a year or two. His self-confidence was almost nonexistent. He told of being the middle of three children born to parents who dreamed of their children becoming outstanding athletes. His brother and sister had won medals and honors in several sports. "But I was a nothing. I'm built like an elephant. I've never been good at any sport. I'm only marginal at golf," he said.

Friends could see and appreciate that this man had considerable ability. He wasn't athletically inclined, but his relational skills were unusually fine. Somehow he couldn't see or affirm his own giftedness. He could only see his failure as an athlete.

We have listened to many versions of this life story from our students. These stories involve parents who, for whatever reason, didn't know or respect the individuality of their children.

Other stories which tell of parental understanding, support, and encouragement and undergird the early stages of the development of life potential stand in bold contrast. Adults who as children believed they were known and respected as individuals also speak of being deeply loved by their parents.

Parents must take risks in coming to know and respect their children. There are times as children grow when they do not want to be known by their parents. Keeping secrets with a best friend, putting a "knock-before-you-enter" sign on the bedroom door, spending an allowance "in my way without telling you," writing or receiving a special letter, and insisting on bathroom privacy are examples of specific situations in which children may shut the door on parental knowing. Moms and dads can respect the child by knowing that unless carried to an extreme for an unreasonable period of time these are normal experiences.

Knowing and respecting need to work together in the parenting process. Rather than being an expression of love, knowing without respecting can deteriorate into domination. Many times dominating parents use their knowledge for illegitimate power and their control to meet their own needs. Respecting without knowing can result in irresponsible parenting. In cases involving drug abuse, alcoholism, and sexual promiscuity, parents may say, "We just didn't know. We had no idea. We were trying to respect our child's right to privacy." Knowledge assists parents in realizing when children need to be held accountable for their actions. Accountability needs to operate in the context of respect, but respect should not be allowed to block parents from holding a child accountable for just and reasonable behavior.

Knowing and respecting our children is important to the task of qualitative parenting. As knowing and respecting grow so does a healthy climate wherein faith can be nurtured.

Forgiving

God's forgiving love is seen most clearly in the cross. God chose to love rather than to judge and condemn. With God's love as a model for healthy relationships wherein faith is encouraged to grow, forgiveness becomes a critical factor in family love. Brokenness pervades the world in which we live. Given the best of intentions, there is still no way we can live side by side in our families without needing forgiveness from one another.

When our daughter was young she used to ask "what if" questions. One of her questions was: "What if we were perfect just like God? We wouldn't make any mistakes, would we?"

The reality is that we are not and cannot be God to one another. We live together with all of our humanness. We are "earthen vessels" (2 Corinthians 4:7, RSV). We do and say things that contribute to brokenness. We omit acting and speaking in ways that would contribute to growth, and fractured relationships result. Sometimes our intentions seem lofty enough, but they are off target in terms of the relationship. Our human limitations can keep us from being all that we would like to be to one another. We need forgiveness from the members of our family. They need forgiveness from us.

We believe that forgiveness is a dialogical process in which the persons involved examine the wrongs that have been done in light of the relationship. How did these things happen? How did each of us contribute to what happened? What can we learn from these situations? How can we keep from repeating them? How can we let go of the wrongs done to us so that they don't become a relational weapon? What does it mean for us to have a fresh start?

If these kinds of questions are addressed, persons can be free to approach one another feeling confident that forgiveness really means changed lives and a fresh start in the family. If forgiveness happens, the fresh start will mean that the incident will no longer be used in hurtful ways. The persons may continue to learn from the experience, but they will follow through on a commitment to discard it as a relational weapon.

Forgiving in Marriage

Marriage is a long-term commitment. If forgiveness becomes part of the relational dynamics between a wife and a husband, they can expand their knowledge of each other and deepen their intimacy. In relationships where forgiveness tends not to happen, hurt and pain begin to accumulate. Resentment and blaming increase, and the marriage feels like a heavy burden. There is no joy.

In cases where a superficial ritual consistently replaces the more extensive process we have described, forgiveness loses its meaning.

"I'm sorry," she mutters tentatively.

"I guess it's okay," he begrudgingly responds. Two weeks later the same kind of incident which led to this encounter repeats itself. She becomes more tentative; he, more begrudging. In between they have handled many other things in a similar manner. They grow ever more alienated from each other.

Forgiveness is a complex dynamic in human relationships. The issues involved can be very difficult. Who initiates the process? When? What if the same wrong is committed again and again? Does one ever draw the line on forgiveness? What if the other person avoids the process? Can forgiveness happen by taking the event to God in prayer rather than approaching the other person? Should a person participate in the process even though she or he does not at all desire to change the behavior? How can we rebuild the trust that has been broken? How much of forgiving my spouse involves forgiving myself?

Each of these questions must be answered in the context of mutual commitment in an intimate relationship. None of the questions are easily answered.

We have been encouraged by a couple who were married for over forty years. The wife observed, ''We've had a long, hard walk. Some times have been harder than others. I really believe that if we made it this far any couple can make it if they want to.'' When we asked how they had done it, she continued, ''Well, we've worked at it. We've had to handle a lot of problems. We've made a lot of mistakes, but there's been a lot of forgiveness.''

While forgiveness may not totally heal the pain in every relationship, it provides a rich resource which goes a long way. Working to establish goals of forgiveness assures the presence of therapeutic healing dimensions in the marital relationship.

Forgiving in Parenting

Parenting is a long walk which once begun lasts a lifetime. Just as in marriage, the forgiveness process is demanding and the issues are complicated in parenting. We want to address some of the issues which seem to surface most frequently and most urgently among parents in the groups where we have taught.

While it is an important ritual to teach children to say ''I'm sorry!'' in appropriate situations, we believe they should move beyond that somewhat simple formula. As children grow older, the parenting task becomes one of helping them see that the words ''I'm sorry'' are really symbolic of their willingness to change their behavior. The words are not a magic phrase which they pronounce to get someone off their backs while they have no intention of changing anything about their behavior.

There are times when children do or say things that bring great pain to parents while the child appears to have no feelings of remorse. The child's seemingly callous attitude adds to the hurt. Before choosing a response it is usually helpful if parents try to identify what is going on from the child's point of view given their limited years of life experience.

One mother told of her experience when her son was three. He suddenly turned to her and screamed, "I hate you, Mommy!" The mother was deeply hurt. "I don't know why. God must have been with me, but I took some time to think what life had been like for him recently. I had been pregnant. Then I went to the hospital, and several days later we brought home a new baby sister. Life hadn't been easy for him. There had been a lot of changes. I decided to go easy with him. When he screamed that he hated me, I felt very sad; I told him how much I loved him. He never did it again. I'm glad I didn't make a big issue out of it!"

One of the most powerful ways children learn to forgive others is through experiencing a parent who asks for forgiveness. "I'm sorry, I made a mistake." "Forgive me, I expected too much from you." "I'm sorry, I was clumsy; I didn't intend to knock into you." "Forgive me, I should have been there for your school program. I can see that now." Parenting is not easy. There are many times when hurt and brokenness come as a result of parental action. These are the times to ask forgiveness. Children can understand the humanness of their parents. It helps them understand and accept their own.

A vivid memory Jan holds of her father is when he came into her room, tears streaming down his cheeks, his voice broken. "Janet, I'm so sorry. I just ran over your pup with the car. I didn't mean to. I should have looked, but I forgot. I'm so sorry." This particular collie pup had been special because she was deaf. Her death was a temporary blow to a ten-year-old. The apology from her father followed up by assistance with proper burial and decisions related to a new puppy have provided lifetime memories of a precious relational gift.

Parents often struggle with self-forgiveness. "If only I had done something differently. . . ." "If I had been there. . . ." "If I would have kept my mouth closed. . . ." "Maybe I should have said something. . . ." There are times we would like to erase a situation and do it all over again.

We have found that accepting our own limitations is crucial. No matter what we would like to be, we cannot be all things to our children. If we accept our own limitations, we provide our children with living portraits of humanness. If we have faithfully tried and fallen short, then we have been obedient parenting stewards. We can ask for forgiveness from God, our children, and ourselves.

Establishing a Faith-Nurturing Climate Based on the Model of God's Love

Care and responsiveness, giving and receiving, accountability, knowing and respecting, and forgiving are interdependent love factors that need to be recognized and implemented if families are to relate to one another in ways which create the kind of context and climate where persons grow toward wholeness and where faith can be optimally nurtured. God's abiding love will be present among us as we commit ourselves to growth in living faithfully as a community of love in our families.

Questions for Reflection and Discussion

1. What have you learned about caring and responding to the various members of your family?

2. What relational experiences in your life would validate the idea that accountability is essential in qualitative relationships?

3. How well do you balance the love factors of giving and receiving in your relationships?

4. What has your life in families taught you about the values of knowing and respecting in creating qualitative relationships?

5. To what degree have your family members learned to be forgiving of one another?

5

Developing Trustworthy Relationships in the Family

God's love would never have been believable if it had been capricious—present at one time and absent at another. Human love which is mercurial in the same way is unbelievable as well.

No doubt the covenantal love of God has been so tremendously enduring and powerful in the lives of the faithful precisely because of its trustworthiness. Indeed, God's covenant with humanity consists of two complementary traits: caring love and trustworthy faithfulness. The Lord is a trustworthy God. The importance of this attribute becomes clear within the context of the covenant and its promises.

> Yahweh your God is God,
> the God worthy of trust
> who keeps His covenant of love forever
> with those who love Him.
> (Deuteronomy 7:9)[1]

All fifty-two verses of Psalm 89 are devoted to praising the steadfast love of a trustworthy God.

In establishing a covenant with humanity God expects us to respond by demonstrating love and trustworthiness in our relationships with God and neighbor. These divine traits provide the foundation upon which to build the attitudinal and behavioral structures for nurturing faith within Christian families.

In the previous chapter we provided insight into how divine love can be implemented in family relationships. In this chapter our goal is to show how families can develop trust for the purpose of faith nurturing by establishing an enduring climate where love is consistent and believable. Our discussion focuses upon five questions related to the theme

70

of this chapter: How important is trust to the family? Is trust related to nurturing faith? What is a definition of trust? How is trust created and maintained? How hard is trust to obtain and maintain?

How Important Is Trust to the Family?

Generally, in healthy families, the members are expected to interact with one another in trustworthy ways. Such trustworthiness creates a climate of stability and harmony where people thrive. In families where there is increased breaking of trust, the result is a climate of rancor and discord.

Recently, two studies of significance have pointed to the importance of trust within the family. One is related to long-term marriages and the other to healthy families.

Trust and Healthy Married Relationships

In 1972 James R. Hine, a professor of family relations and a marital therapist, began a study designed to look at the health and well-being of marriages over a number of years. He has taken an intensive look at fifty couples, measuring growth and change in their marriages through the years. Two questions have interested him in his studies.

> (1) What are the ingredients of a healthy, happy marriage, and do all competent marriages share certain basic characteristics? (2) How do couples meet the changes that come into their lives over the years, and what does it take to grow through change in positive directions toward fulfilling rewards?[2]

A number of characteristics of healthy marriages emerged. First and foremost were dependability and trustworthiness. Next was mutual respect and third were loyalty and faithfulness.[3] Trust in a marriage really cannot exist without mutual respect and loyalty.

In reviewing what marriage partners in the study said about each other, Hine found the word "trust" being used time after time. If a marriage relationship is to be healthy, rewarding, and satisfying, an abiding trust in one's spouse is a necessity. Where there is mutual trust there is a solid feeling that all is well and the future of the marriage will be good. Trust is both a gift spouses give to each other and a feeling based on past experiences that one's mate is dependable and predictable.[4]

Trust and Healthy Families

In 1983 family specialist and author Dolores Curran reported the results of a survey that she conducted with professionals who work with families. The professionals consisted of teachers, doctors, principals, pastors, religious educators, Boy Scout directors, YMCA leaders, Big Brothers, 4-H leaders, family counselors, and others who work closely with families. Her data is based upon the responses of 551 professionals. She asked them to check fifteen items out of fifty-six which they thought were characteristic of healthy families.

According to these professionals trait #4 is: ''The healthy family develops a sense of trust.'' Traits 1-3 are:

> ''The healthy family
> 1. communicates and listens.
> 2. affirms and supports one another.
> 3. teaches respect for others.'' [5]

It is hard to imagine trustworthy families not exhibiting the above three characteristics, for these behaviors contribute strongly to trust in human relationships.

In the healthy family trust is a precious possession that is carefully developed and nurtured as both children and parents progress together through the various life and family cycles. Tragically, in some families one can never be certain about trusting other members.

> Are they really loved, or are they merely tolerated because they happen to belong to the family? Can they trust their parents (or children) to do what they do because they *love* them? Can they be sure of anyone? Will they still be seeking security and love at age eighty?[6]

In the healthy family the marital partners work on being trustworthy to each other. Husbands and wives want to be trusted by their mate to be faithful in love. Together they seek to develop a trustworthy family climate with their children. They can be counted upon to be present as loving, caring parents whenever their children need them. They expect their children to be trustworthy in their relationships with other family members. Trust in family relations is a basic ingredient to family health.

Is Trust Related to Nurturing Faith?

Trust is essential to the emergence of religious faith. The noted psychoanalyst Erik Erikson in his many works has demonstrated the inextricable interrelationship of trust and faith. Faith is possible only to the extent that trust and hope have developed in the life of the person. The religious dimension pervades the various stages of life development; however, this dimension is profoundly affected by how trustworthy early parenting figures have been in a person's life.[7] More will be said about the importance of trust as the foundation for developing faith below and in chapter 6.

A leading theoretician on trust, Jack R. Gibb, also highlights the importance of trust to the life of faith. He writes, "Trust provides an environment that nourishes personal growth, holistic health, spirituality, and the discovery of the soul." [8] Gibb believes that life could be greatly enhanced if our spirituality was integrated into all aspects of living. It is his conviction that as persons develop trust they gradually transcend the barriers that keep them from achieving their full spirituality. As persons get in touch with and grow in trust, self-integration and a sense of wholeness with reality emerges.[9]

Earlier we referred to a study on the formation of faith by Gordon E. Jackson. In his study of 210 persons of faith he discovered that 85 percent of them grew up in homes of integrity. These were not always Christian homes. In the case of one of his subjects the home had no religious orientation at all. However, the subject spoke of the deep integrity in his home. Jackson concluded that these families of his subjects provided a trustworthy climate in which their children grew. Their faith took root in the form of basic trust. According to Jackson, trust is the earliest and most pervasive form of faith.[10]

The Dynamics of Trust in Nurturing Faith

How does trust contribute to the nurturing of faith? What are the psychological dynamics related to trust that shape faith within humans?

To understand the dynamics of trust and its role in faith nurturing, it is important to understand that the opposite of trust is fear. The presence or absence of trust or fear can make a powerful difference in our lives. They are primary and catalytic forces in all human living, including our faith relationship with God.

Trust enriches life; fear terrorizes it. Trust releases the growth processes within persons whereas fear constrains and blocks these processes. Trust energizes the flow of the growth processes. Feeling and thinking are focused and mobilized. Consciousness is awakened; openness to maturation is created. Psychological processes like feeling, imagination, creativity, awareness, courage, intuition, playfulness, risk taking, and energy are released and growth occurs. On the other hand, fear stagnates the growth processes. Feeling and thinking are mobilized defensively rather than creatively. Consciousness is restricted, and openness to growth and change is reduced. The psychological processes become unfocused, divided, and destructive. When trust is high, persons can move toward wholeness. When fear is high, persons can become fragmented and even psychotic. Trust engenders trust in self, others, and God. Trust unleashes growth energy in all of life's important spheres. On the other hand, fear creates doubt, suspicion, and mistrust of self, others, and God.

One man in his late thirties told of the lack of trust in his home. His father worked as a long-distance truck driver. His father visited home erratically and was often sour and abusive to his mother and the children. The mother worked at unskilled domestic jobs when she could find them, leaving the children to care for themselves. The family atmosphere was negative and hostile.

"I think I was afraid every hour of the day as a child. I was afraid of my father. I was afraid of my mother. She seemed so frail to me, and I saw her working so hard. I was afraid my brothers would do something wrong, and I would get blamed. Punishment in our home was cruel."

He went on to describe how his fears had continued to dominate his life. He was fearful of close relationships, but terrified he might be without them. He had great fear of failing but also a fear of succeeding. It seemed that no matter which way he turned fear stared back at him. "I really haven't gone anywhere with my life. I've even been afraid of God. Somehow I've been afraid God would never help me. God's always given me such a raw deal in life."

In contrast to fear, trust among family members creates a basic trustworthiness of life and of God, the Source of life. Upon the foundation of such trust, commitments can be made to oneself, others, and God. Both the trustworthiness of God and of those created in the divine image make possible one's ability to make lasting commitments—the essence of Christian discipleship.

On the toy chest in our basement is a beautiful rag doll with long, black, yarn braids, a frilly red dress with a ruffled petticoat, and satin slippers. Although our children have enjoyed her, it is "Mom's" doll. Jan has an interesting story about Maria Doll II.

When Jan was four, her birthday present was a magnificent rag doll, almost as tall as she was, dressed in a red dress. Jan's mother had somehow managed to make the doll on the treadle sewing machine without Jan's knowledge.

Maria Doll went everywhere with the active farm girl—to bed, the cellar, the hayloft, the chicken coop, the tree house, and for a quick spin down the lane in the bicycle basket. Gradually the newness wore off. There were dirty smudges on Maria Doll's face and hands. The dress had been torn in a few places. The yarn hair was in disarray.

When Jan was seven she had scarlet fever and was confined to bed for several weeks. The house was under quarantine. Maria Doll was Jan's constant companion.

Following the illness everything had to be disinfected or thrown away. Mom Duncan tried to decide what to do about the doll. "Janet, we have to do something with Maria Doll," Mom Duncan said. She listed several alternatives—none of which helped Jan make a choice. "If you don't choose, I'll do it for you," Mom Duncan warned. In Jan's mind it was "no choice" whatever decision was made. Maria Doll would never be the same!

One day Maria Doll disappeared. "I burned her," Mom Duncan explained. "The doctor thought it was best. Dad and I agreed with him. I'm sorry you had scarlet fever. I'm sorry about the doll. It's just not safe to take chances. You have been very sick."

Jan was devastated. Her mother gave her a new baby doll which received much attention, but rarely left the house and never visited the hayloft or the tree house.

Nearly two years later Jan's Christmas presents included a huge, lumpy, tissue-wrapped package. On the package was a note.

Dear Janet,

I felt bad about burning Maria Doll. I know it made you feel very sad. It's taken me a long time to make another one. I couldn't find the same material for her dress, but it is close. I think her braids are a bit longer. I couldn't remember what color to make her eyes, so I made them blue-gray like yours. I hope you like her.

I love you.
Mommy

Other activities were more important to a nine-year-old than playing with a doll. Maria Doll II sat on the bed at home and later at college. She was carefully packed away in a storage box when we lived in our early tiny apartments. Today she sits on our toy chest—a beautiful reminder of restored trust and integrity in family relationships.

An essential aspect of nurturing faith is developing and maintaining a high level of trust among family members. Given that this is the case, let's now take a deeper look at trust by examining the last three questions upon which this chapter is organized.

What Is a Definition of Trust?

To take a deeper look at trust as the basis for faith nurturing, let's begin by defining "trust." What is it like to trust another human being? When are we being trusting and when are we not being trusting? When are we behaving in a trustworthy way and when are we violating the trust of someone else? How do we recognize trust when we see or experience it? "Trust" is a commonly used word, and everyone knows something of its meaning. However, it is a very complex idea and difficult to capture within the confines of words.

Webster provides a definition of trust that is relevant to this discussion. Trust is ". . . reliance on the character, ability, strength, or truth of someone or something." *The American Heritage Dictionary* has a similar definition: "Firm reliance on the integrity, ability, or character of a person. . . ."

Trust may be defined as consisting of the following features:

1. *Risk*—a person is in a situation in which a choice to trust another can lead to either beneficial or harmful consequences for one's needs and goals.
2. *Dependence*—one realizes that whether the results are good or bad depends upon the future action of another person.
3. *Loss/gain*—one expects to lose much more if trust is violated than one would gain if one's trust is fulfilled.
4. *Confidences*—one feels confident that the other will act in such a manner that the beneficial consequences will result.[11]

Thus parents who leave their baby with a sitter make a trusting choice. They are aware that their choice could lead to good or bad results depending upon the action of the baby-sitter. They realize they would suffer much more if their trust in the baby-sitter was misplaced (and the baby was hurt) than they would gain if their trust was well-founded (they are free for a night out). Yet they put their trust in the baby-sitter because they feel confident that he or she will act in such a way that the results will be beneficial.

How Is Trust Created and Maintained?

The Importance of Trust to the Growing Infant

Human beings are gifted with developing capacities for faith. How these capacities are triggered and emerge is dependent largely on how we are welcomed into our families of origin and what kinds of nurturing environments they provide.

Erikson indicates that a primary need of infants under the age of two is nurturing. Through the nurturing process a baby develops the capacity to trust or to mistrust. If the nurturing has been done with acceptance and caring, trust emerges. If the nurturing has been neglectful and hurtful, mistrust develops. The first step in nurturing faith in the family is to surround newborns with parents and others who lovingly care for the infant. With such care the infant child learns to trust her or his environment. The importance of trust and its relationship to faith nurturance will be further developed in chapter 6 of this book.

Characteristics, Attitudes, and Behaviors Necessary for Building Trustworthy Family Climates

There is much that can be done to create trust within families and between family members beyond nurturing the newborn. The creation of trustworthy climates calls for a collage of personal characteristics and attitudes as well as behavioral skills. What follows is an identification and explication of these characteristics, attitudes, and behaviors that lead to trust as well as mistrust.

The "Conceptual Framework for Trusting Relationships" table presents various personal characteristics, attitudes, and behaviors that contribute to a climate of trust in the family. The table also presents those traits that promote a family environment of mistrust.

These twenty-two positive items demonstrate the claim that trust is complex. It is complex because there is much involved in making it come to pass. All of these positive characteristics, attitudes, and behaviors do not have to be present within family living for trust to exist. However, the trust level will depend on the degree to which they are present. Mistrust will be present to the degree that the negative characteristics, attitudes, and behaviors are present.

Perhaps a brief look at each of the items will help fix them in your understanding. *Personal characteristics* and *attitudes* form the first set of factors which contribute to a trustworthy climate.

Open versus closed. Open persons are willing to share their innermost thoughts and feelings with family members. Of course, closed persons are just the opposite; they keep their thoughts and feelings to themselves. Every family member has a need for thoughts and aspects of their lives that they do not share. However, life can become very difficult when information needed for effective family living is being deliberately kept from others. Shared information contributes to trust between members.

A Conceptual Framework for Trusting Relationships

Trust in family relationships   Mistrust in family relationships

is created and maintained

when these personal *characteristics* and

attitudes are present

Open	Closed
Supportive	Controlling
Willing to risk	Unwilling to risk
Caring	Hostile
Genuine	Hypocritical
Cooperative	Competitive
Mutual	Superior
Problem-centered	Solution-minded
Accepting and warm	Rejecting and cold
Dependable	Capricious
Relationally competent	Relationally incompetent

Trust in family relationships   Mistrust in family relationships

is created and maintained

when these *behaviors* are present

Initiates	Waits
Establishes eye contact	Avoids eye contact
Communicates clearly	Communicates obscurely
Gives and receives feedback	Communicates one-way
Listens emphathically	Listens defensively
Expresses personal feelings	Withholds personal feelings
Accepts feelings	Rejects feelings
Uses "I" messages	Uses "You" messages
Affirms the other's self-image	Deprecates the other's self-image
Is present, involved	Is absent, detached
Appreciates the other's trust	Fails to acknowledge the other's trust

If family members are to create a climate of trust, they must be appropriately open with each other and practice the art of disclosing inner thoughts and feelings.

Supportive versus controlling. The supportive person seeks to be encouraging, reassuring, and understanding of other family members and their agendas and goals. The controlling person tries to bind other family members to his or her desires and wishes. This member operates on the assumption that other members are inadequate and need to be dominated by someone who has it "together." Supportiveness creates a climate of trust; control engenders a climate of resistance and defensiveness. It is easy to trust persons who support you. A supportive attitude among family members contributes to a trustworthy climate in which faith can be nurtured.

Willing to risk versus unwilling to risk. To trust another person is a risky action. A decision to trust can lead to either good or bad consequences. Family living surely entails this type of risk taking. To entrust one's well-being to other family members makes a person very vulnerable. Risking is the process of deciding to accept potentially adverse results that may come from trusting another. The greater the risk involved, the more one is required to trust another. Taking such risks with other family members tends to create a trusting climate because to risk ourselves with others communicates to them that we trust them. In playing it safe others recognize our unwillingness to trust. Such caution with others fails to generate trust among persons.

Caring versus hostile. It is easy to trust family members when we are convinced that they care for us deeply and love us completely. On the other hand, it is very difficult to trust those who are intentionally hurtful. Knowing that other family members are concerned about our well-being and growth goes a long way in helping us to believe that the risks of trust are worth it. If we begin to doubt that others love and care for us and begin to experience either apathy or hate, we may feel ourselves becoming more and more mistrusting of others. In families where physical abuse takes place the power of fear overwhelms the bonds of trust and impedes psychological and spiritual growth. Caring family members look out for one another's welfare and thereby create a home climate filled with trust and love.

Genuine versus hypocritical. The genuine person is a person of integrity. The importance of integrity to trust is clearly pointed out in Webster's definition of trust which we quoted previously. The genuine person's thoughts, feelings, and actions are consistent. It is very difficult to trust a family member when we experience a discrepancy among his or her words, emotions, and conduct. We can never be certain about the meaning of their words, about their true intentions, or about what they are going to do. We experience such persons as being hypocritical. The genuine person is an honest person. Trusting such persons comes easily because we experience them for who they say they are. Indeed, they say what they mean; they clarify their intentions; they follow through on their promises.

Cooperative versus competitive. A cooperative attitude builds trust whereas a competitive attitude feeds mistrust. When a spirit of cooperation pervades a family, relevant information is shared openly, clearly, and honestly. In competitive families communication is either lacking or misleading. Cooperation requires teamwork to achieve common goals. Competition calls for achieving personal objectives at the expense of other family members. To the competitive family member, individual goals are more important than group goals. Whenever a competitive spirit pervades the family climate, trust may be difficult to achieve and fear and defensiveness are the likely result. On the other hand, the give and take of cooperation creates a fellowship of trust among family members.

Mutual versus superior. When family members communicate that they feel superior in some way to others, a climate of mistrust and defensiveness is assured. When members of the family indicate a willingness to cooperate, mutual trust, respect, and an environment of openness and trustworthiness result. Mutuality seeks to resolve issues in family living through shared problem solving. There is a desire for two-way communication. Power is shared. Status is minimized; personhood is maximized. Each person's self-worth is valued. A spirit of mutuality generates a trustworthy climate in which each person's journey of faith is respected and nurtured.

Problem-centered versus solution-minded. Persons with a problem-centered attitude seek a collaborative effort in defining family problems, exploring alternatives, and arriving at solutions. These individuals have no preplanned solutions to impose on the family and its various members. Members of the family are encouraged to set their own goals, make their own decisions, and evaluate their own progress in light of the nature of the problem and the various alternatives open to them in resolving the problem. Other members may listen as one seeks to articulate the problem as he or she sees it; they may also suggest a variety of solutions without providing *the* solution.

Solution-minded persons, on the other hand, operate on the assumption that simply because a family or personal problem has been recognized it is understood. They are quick to arrive at solutions and fail to explore the nature of the problem. They often have a strong tendency to impose their answers upon other family members. Adopting an immediate-solution approach tends to generate negative feelings, a divisive climate, and an atmosphere of endless argumentation and fruitless debate. Nurturing families will strive to be problem-centered people, for this characteristic builds trust and provides a context for faith maturation.

Accepting and warm versus rejecting and cold. An accepting and warm attitude is a major contributor to trust-building. On the other hand, a rejecting and cold attitude creates feelings of rejection, low self-esteem, and hostility that lead to mistrust and suspicion. Accepting attitudes lead to feelings of psychological safety. Such attitudes contribute to feelings that no matter what one discloses about oneself, the other person or persons in the family will respond in an accepting, nonjudgmental manner. Warmth in family relationships is absolutely essential to creating a trustworthy climate for growth in faith. When an attitude of warmth is communicated among family members, people feel prized for who they are and what they have to contribute to family living.

Dependable versus capricious. Probably the most critical characteristic related to the creation of trust is dependability. Over and over again it has been shown that we will trust others more easily and more deeply if we believe we can rely on them. Our trust will be more widespread if we can predict how other family members will respond—even in small things like being on time for a meal, putting away shoes so that others won't stumble over them, and showing appreciation for what others do. Dependability is important to building trust.

Predictability emerges from dependability. If we can depend on one another time after time, we learn that we can predict one another's behavior in many situations. Because we can rely on one another and predict much of our behavior, we feel safe in trusting our family. In life-shaking events we predict and rely on trustworthy relationships in the family. A teenage son who has wrecked the family car trusts he will be treated fairly. A young adult daughter trusts she will have freedom to leave home and establish an independent life. A husband and wife in the midst of a heated argument trust that the conflict will not lead to rejection. On the other hand, capriciousness leads to unpredictability and mistrust. Capricious family members cannot be depended upon, and their behavior creates confusion and chaos in daily living. This results in mistrust.

Relationally competent versus relationally incompetent. Research in interpersonal trust indicates that human beings trust people who are knowledgeable and competent in the area in which trust is to be given.[12] We don't trust those who have little or no knowledge of what they are talking about. What does all this mean for family living? There will be a high trust level in families where all members are well-informed about the dynamics of family living and where family members have or are developing relational skills that contribute to trust-building. When family members do not understand the dynamics of family living in general and theirs in particular, they often blame one another for what feels wrong. When relational skills are missing, many bad communication dynamics can be generated that lead to a very hostile, defensive climate. Such climates contribute little or nothing to faith nurturing.

Behaviors form the second set of factors which contribute to creating and maintaining a trustworthy climate. These are interpersonal actions that help to build trust in the family. Again there are eleven sets of behaviors.

Initiates versus waits. Can you imagine a family where everyone waits for the others to take action or to start conversation? Why would a family behave in such a manner? One cue may be that there is a serious trust problem among family members. We initiate conversation and action with others based upon some degree of trust in them. If our trust is unwarranted because they have hurt or punished us for what we've done, we may very well become one of the waiters rather than one of the initiators in family living. When we initiate any communication or action with others, we are placing a degree of trust in them. If we initiate deep self-revelation or take highly risky action, we are placing a high-level of trust in other family members. Such trust does not go unnoticed; it is often returned by another family member's trustworthy action. Initiators expect other family members to be trustworthy. Fortunately, human beings tend to conform to expectations others have of them. Trust is often returned to the initiator of trust. At that point trust becomes mutual and trust building occurs in the family.

Establishes eye contact versus avoids eye contact. Establishing eye contact is an important ingredient to building trust in our society.[13] A person who avoids eye contact is often seen as having something to hide. Dishonesty in communication is often associated with the inability to make and maintain eye contact. Mutual eye contact is the purest form of interpersonal give and take. The eye cannot receive information from others without, at the same time, conveying information to others. Eye contact is critical to family trust, for this form of contact has a way of bonding family members together into a cohesive unit. To avoid eye contact is to cause members of the family to feel devalued at very deep levels, for in our society it is the most powerful way of saying to someone that he or she does not exist in that person's world. It is impossible to trust someone who does not acknowledge your existence.

Communicates clearly versus communicates obscurely. Clarity in communication builds trust whereas unclear messages create confusion and mistrust. The importance of clear, accurate communication can hardly be overemphasized in family living. This includes everything from who's to take out the garbage to how to convey our love for family members. When communication becomes muddled, tangential, or distorted, we often blame one another for what's gone wrong rather than seeing that the problem lies in our faulty communication. When the dynamics of blaming and accusing get started, it takes its toll on trust building in the family. Trust building is aided when family members work for clear, accurate communication with one another. As a result, faith nurturing is also aided.

Gives and receives feedback versus communicates one-way. If communication is one-way in the family, trust building is very difficult. Indeed, the task of trust building rests upon the shoulders of the primary communicator in the family—most likely the mother or the father. When family members are able to give and receive corrective feedback, communication becomes more flexible. The flexibility of such dialogical communication makes possible the creation of trust. One-way communication has a rigid structure that tends to undercut trust dynamics.

Listens empathically versus listens defensively. Listening is probably one of the most important relational skills we can adopt for building family trust. Learning to be an empathic listener is especially important. Such an approach to listening integrates physical, emotional, and intellectual abilities in an active search for understanding what another person is saying. Because the empathic listener seeks to see the world from the other's viewpoint, it is a powerful trust-building force. On the other hand, defensive listening has the opposite effect. The defensive listener tunes into what another family member is saying only to judge it as inadequate and to point out the flaws in what the person has revealed. Listening time is used to build one's own case against what is being presented by another person. Such an approach to listening tears at the fabric of family trust in a very harmful way. Such a climate allows little room for faith nurturing to occur.

Expresses personal feelings versus withholds personal feelings. Expressing our feelings to other family members is an act of trust and therefore builds trust in the family. To share our emotional life with other family members is risky business, especially in a family where the climate is hostile and untrustworthy. The entrustment of one's own feelings into the care of others is a deeply personal act. Our emotional life is intensely personal and when shared with others conveys that we trust them. When we withhold our feelings from other family members, we communicate mistrust and fear of them. We don't trust them enough to share our private selves, for we fear that they may judge, ridicule, laugh at, or ignore the feelings we share. It's simply safer to withhold our personal feelings rather than risk such hurt.

Accepts feelings versus rejects feelings. This behavior is closely related to the accepting/rejecting attitude discussed previously. It is important to welcome the feelings of others. Trust as well as personal and interpersonal growth occur when feelings are mutually shared and received. Positive human growth and development require the exploration of our feelings. When our feelings are blocked from being expressed, growth is stifled. It is important to have someone ready and willing to accept our feelings when we express them. Trust comes easily when there are persons in our family to accept our most private feelings. Trust is impossible when family members reject one another's expressed feelings. Acceptance of feelings is a critical behavior in building family trust; it provides rich soil for faith in God to take root, be nurtured, and grow.

Uses "I" messages versus uses "You" messages. The English language uses pronouns in terms of first, second, and third persons. In family communication the third person is used for objective description of reality. The second person "you" may be used for commands: "You clean the bathtub, now!" Often it is used in an evaluative way: "You are too pushy for this family." Such communication comes across as being from on high. Behind it lies some kind of moral imperative—a message that you ought to be this way or you ought not be this way. Such communication is experienced as being a judgment about one's opinions, feelings, motives, or behaviors—indeed, about one's whole person. The first person "I" is used to make personal statements. It states the way things are from my point of view: "I would appreciate your cleaning the bathroom right now" or "I really think you are a pushy person." To use "I" personalizes communication. Such communication builds trust between persons because I speak for myself and no one else. "I" messages become less threatening to others when a person speaks from one's experience. For example, ''I experience you as a pushy person'' has a different tone than ''I really think you are a pushy person.'' ''I'' language positively affects trust building in the family.

Affirms the other's self-image versus deprecates the other's self-image. Behavior that affirms another's self-image creates a climate of trust, whereas behavior that deprecates another's self-image generates a defensive environment. Affirming and appreciating the best in others bring forth the conditions that make for trust building. Such affirmation causes a feeling of self-appreciation that makes possible trust in others. When persons feel put down by other family members, they can feel only hurt and anger. Trust is the furthest thing from their minds. Feelings of getting even are more likely. If they choose to act on such feelings, the action only contributes to the deprecation of others and the undermining of a trustworthy climate in the family.

Being present, involved versus being absent, detached. Being present and available is critical to building a trustworthy climate in the family. Trust is the result of interaction processes in the family. For such interaction to occur family members have to be present to communicate with one another. Absent figures communicate little or nothing, and certainly nothing that contributes to trust among family members. Indeed, a member who is absent from the family without reason may create a great deal of suspicion among other members as to what he or she is doing with their time. Closely related to presence is involvement. One can be present in the family but hidden behind a book or lost in a television program. Such detachment or ''present but absent'' style of family living contributes little or nothing to family trust. Being actively involved in the family and its various activities generates trust within the family.

Appreciates the other's trust versus fails to acknowledge the other's trust. One of the quickest ways to build trust in family relationships is to show appreciation for the trust others have placed in you. On the other hand, being unappreciative can undercut the trustworthy efforts of other members of the family. Trust grows slowly, and it deepens as each person becomes involved in the process. If one has shared a significant part of oneself with another family member, one waits for a response. An act of trust by one family member has the strong potential of creating acts of trust from the others. When trust giving and trust appreciation are mutual, a trustworthy climate for faith nurturing in the family is well in the making.

The Nurturing of Trust

It should be clear by now that trust building involves a complex set of attitudes, characteristics, and behaviors. Yet trust is essential to family health and to faith nurturing. Trust must be nurtured and maintained if Christian families are to enjoy their life together and to grow in their faith relationship with Jesus Christ.

What do we as family members need to do to develop and sustain trust? One insight we need to understand clearly is that trust building takes hard work, considerable time and energy, and also involves risk. The challenge is to become trustworthy persons to one another, constantly investing the time and energy it takes and being willing to take the risk.

To nurture trust we must be trustworthy ourselves. We need to be all that we can be as persons worthy of trust within the family. If trust is to grow and deepen, family members will be required to continue earning the right to be trusted. By seeking to embody many of the attitudes, characteristics, and behaviors cited above, we will earn that right.

How Hard Is Trust to Obtain and Maintain?

Trust in Our World

Trust appears to be a universally acknowledged human attitude. It is the basis of human relationships; it grounds much of intellectual thought and scientific research. It provides the fundamental reason for acting according to ethical norms of loving service. It is also the reason we live out a faithful relationship to the triune God. Indeed, trust is foundational to much of our life experience.

Yet, if we look at the history of human thinking from the radical doubt of Descartes to the nihilism of much of modern philosophy, we discover that this fundamental human attitude is a rare commodity. According to Carolyn Gratton, a psychologist and professor of spirituality, many people are aware that something is seriously amiss in contemporary society because there seems to be a blatant inability on the part of most North Americans to live in trustworthy ways.[14]

Jack Gibb, another psychologist, writes, ". . . our present national culture—social, economic, even artistic, as well as political—is inhospitable to trust." [15] Gibb also points out that, unhappily, trust is not a part of the global scene either. A look at various terrorist activities around the world and the displacement of people from their homes and their countries quickly provides us a picture of mistrust and fear.

Trust does not come naturally. For trust to happen in our families, we must want it and work for it. Global and cultural realities are against us; they do not reinforce our efforts at trust building. Faith-nurturing families will need to be a countercultural force advocating and striving for trustworthy attitudes and behaviors in their families as well as in the larger culture.

Difficult to Achieve

Trust is difficult to achieve. We must work hard to obtain it, for trust grows slowly. Because of the complexity of trust; it can't be built in a day. It takes time, relational time.

One young couple met through their common employment in the same organization. As weeks went by they dated and their relationship began to deepen. There came a point when they spoke of marriage. They found there were major trust issues to be discussed and hurdled. In the work place both had witnessed the other treating persons in ways they did not want to be treated in their marriage. They had to spend many hours exploring whether they could develop the depth of mutual trust both desired in their marriage. It took several months for them to arrive at the point where they could affirm their trust and commit themselves to marriage.

Years later, after their wedding, after having two children, and after establishing a business of their own, they looked back on that period of trust building and observed: ''It took a lot of time. It was very hard work, but it was worth it. We knew then and we know now that we can trust each other.''

Even when trust has become deep and strong in a family relationship, it can be demolished as quickly and easily. One life action, completed within a short time, can erase trust which has taken months, even years to build. When trust is betrayed, hurt, anger, fear, and defensiveness quickly find their place in the drama of family living. We take on self-protecting roles to minimize the pain and the hurt.

In some senses trust is like a vapor. An untrustworthy act can blow it away. Whenever someone betrays our trust, that trust becomes weak and fragile.

Forgiveness and Broken Trust

Because trust is difficult to achieve, it is not unusual for family members to act in untrustworthy ways. We make promises that we can't keep. Despite our good intentions we find ourselves being undependable. Given a stress-filled day, we act out in ways that are rejecting, hostile, and manipulative. We are finite creatures. Our humanity is a broken humanity. The severity of our brokenness is probably never more apparent than it is in the family. Because of our closeness to one another and our knowledge of one another, our human limitations are easily discovered.

So what are we to do? Fortunately, our faith perspectives provide needed help. Deeply embedded in God's promises and Jesus' action is forgiveness for humanity's unfaithfulness. God models forgiveness for us in our broken relationships.

What the process of forgiveness involves has been discussed in chapter 4. However, we do want to highlight that forgiveness is essential to the process of rebuilding broken trust. Trust is very difficult to rebuild when it has been broken. "I trusted once; I took the risk and was hurt; obviously I was naive; I won't trust again." These are rather typical thoughts of a person who feels betrayed in a trusting relationship. As family members we need time, space, support, and forgiving love until the pain lessens, the fears are managed, and we can take another leap of trust. That leap can seem next to impossible for long periods of time. As we have said, initial trust is slow in building. Rebuilding broken trust is even slower. Sometimes in the wake of deep hurt, pain, and anger it never happens. Family members can end up feeling isolated and alienated from themselves, other family members, and God. Forgiving love may be the only force that can penetrate this wall of isolation and alienation.

Called to Trustworthiness

In this chapter we have tried to point out how important trust is to successful family living and how essential it is to nurturing faith. We have also attempted to demonstrate how trust is created and what a complex process it is.

Given the place trust has in nurturing faith, we would like to end this chapter by presenting you a challenge. It's our challenge, too. Each of us is called to trustworthiness in family relationships just as God has been trustworthy to us. Trust is probably tested more in family living than in any other arena of life. If we can pass the test, the result will be strong, enduring family relationships. Another result may be family members who have developed a vital faith in God. To achieve those worthwhile results, it behooves each of us to accept God's call to trustworthiness in our family relationships.

Questions for Reflection and Discussion

1. Can you identify situations in your family or among persons you know where the breaking of trust has led to rancor and discord?

2. How valid is Jack Gibb's concept that as persons develop in trusting they transcend barriers which keep them from achieving their full spirituality?

3. What life examples can you provide that show that fear is a blocking, terrorizing force which stagnates growth in persons?

4. What insights have you gained about trustworthy relationships from studying "A Conceptual Framework for Trusting Relationships"?

5. Which of the personal characteristics, attitudes, and behaviors need to be more present in your family living if trust is to grow? What goals are you willing to set to help trust develop?

PART THREE
The Developmental Context of Faith Nurturing in the Family

6

Faith Nurturing and the Individual Family Member

A faith nurturing climate is built through trustworthy and loving relationships. It can be enhanced by taking into consideration the needs of the individual members of the family as well as the life-cycle stage of the family itself. These are the topics addressed in Part 3. Chapter 6 focuses on the life development of individual persons and how that relates to family faith nurturing. In chapter 7 we consider the interaction between faith nurturing and the cycle of family life.

''Pilgrimage'' is one of the words frequently chosen today to describe the idea that the faith walk continues throughout life. Persons of faith are engaged in a lifelong pilgrimage with God, with other people, and with the created world. Different faith-nurturing challenges must be addressed appropriately to the various stages of the life walk.

One difficulty in describing what faith nurturing in families ought to look like is that individual family members may be at different places in their life walk. Grandmother is seventy-four; Mom and Dad are in their forties; Older Brother is twenty-five and no longer living at home; Older Sister is twenty-one and in college. Younger Sister is seventeen and a senior in high school. Little Brother is nine. Given this mix of ages and needs, what does qualitative faith nurturing look like in this family?

A partial response is that faith nurturing must be broad and rich enough to encompass the needs of persons at all of these age levels. Faith nurturing must be structured so that different persons can relate to it with minimal frustration. It must be flexible enough to change because five years from now the family may look very different from how it looks today.

In some ways and at some levels the faith journeys of all individuals tend to look alike. Scholars and persons working in the helping professions have identified stages that faith pilgrims move through and then return to to pass through again. Each time pilgrims journey through a stage they do so at deeper levels or from new perspectives. Yet each pilgrim's journey is unique because of time, place, and personality.

We (Myron and Jan) have seen Mel and Tim struggle with particular faith issues very much like we did at their ages. We are tempted to think that because we have been there we know precisely what their journeys are like and where they are heading. However, such is not the case.

Today Mel's college world is very different from the one we experienced at the end of the 1950s. Her ways of thinking and feeling are not the same as ours were at her age. She must find the answers which fit her situation. What we perceived as God's direction for us moving into the 1960s may not be the direction God will lead Mel as she attempts to address the complexities in a global village moving toward the 1990s.

Tim has another year before he enters college. His generation will see reality yet differently. His college world will have experienced five years of change from the one Mel entered. In our world of fast-paced progress five years represents considerable change.

When individuals return in their faith pilgrimage to stages they have walked through before, the territory may seem very familiar. However, the persons have changed. They bring more life history to the stage. They will receive new insights and understandings if they are open to learn and to grow.

Faith Development Stages

Before a more detailed consideration of specific faith stages, we will present some principles which underlie a developmental perspective toward faith nurturing. These principles relate to the lifelong process of faith development and some of its complexities.[1]

1. Persons pass through a series of somewhat identifiable stages of faith as they progress through life.

2. Rather specific faith issues and tasks are associated with each stage. While these same issues and tasks may be present during other periods, they gain unusual intensity during certain stages.

3. If the faith issues and tasks of one stage are not dealt with and

mastered to some extent, they act as complicating blockages in later stages.

4. Persons do not necessarily progress to the highest stages in faith development. They may "level off" at a stage where they feel comfortable. They may start to take the initial stages seriously late in life.

5. Movement from one stage to another is usually triggered by some internal or external push or crisis.

6. Individuals move through stages in their own way. Stages of faith development may mean a very different thing for exceptional persons who struggle with severe physical or emotional conditions than they mean to persons not faced with these hardships.

7. Persons may go through certain stages more than once—each time with a new perspective.

Families are likely to do more qualitative faith nurturing if they are aware that family members can be at very different stages of faith development. In the rest of this chapter we will consider some of the faith issues and tasks faced by individuals at different life stages.

Infant Years

Faith, or the seeds of faith development, begins at birth. The newborn is totally dependent on other persons for survival.

We mentioned earlier that faith develops as babies interact with the adults who care for them. The process is rather haphazard and ill-defined in many ways. It goes something like this.

A baby girl lies cooing in her crib. She begins to get vague sensations in her tiny body that something is not well. Her next coo is edged with a whimper. The sensations continue to come—more intense and more constant. Whimpers replace the coos. If something doesn't happen to correct the situation, the baby's involvement will grow more intense. Her whimpers become full-fledged cries. Finally, she wails at a piercingly high pitch. She flails her arms and legs. Her eyes are shut; her face is taut. She is signaling to someone out there that something is very wrong. She needs attention now!

The loving father comes to attend to her needs. Just his presence makes a difference. The pitch of the cries lowers, and the volume decreases dramatically. The arms and legs slow their pace. The eyes fly open and focus intently on Dad's face. Dad initiates the investigation. Need changing? Need turning? Need food or water? Need a change of scenery? Need a pat on the back? Need to be held?

As the baby senses that Dad is really going to do something about those strong and discomforting sensations, she begins to relax. She feels secure and cared for.

During the early months of life this process repeats itself many times. As Dad and Mom consistently and lovingly meet the needs of the baby, she gradually learns a crucial message about trust. Over time she grows confident and trusting that there really is someone out there who cares for and responds to her.

She can't talk about her developing trust. She has no recognizable vocabulary or language structure. She won't bore you with an explanation of why her trust is growing. She has no knowledge of sophisicated psychological theories that explain what is happening. She just *knows* and *trusts* that when something goes wrong with her equilibrium, someone is there to help.

It is not realistic to hold to the belief that parents can or even should meet every need or whim of infants at the moment they want it. The first baby in the family usually teaches parents some important lessons. The baby's fussy message is "I will be walked or rocked all night, thank you! It's a wonderful feeling to be close to you. I like being in motion." A parent's reaction to this message will probably be different when the baby is sick or in a new environment than when he or she is simply registering a preference. Leaving the baby alone for ten to fifteen minutes of protest in the crib may be the most appropriate and loving response parents can make.

The interactions infants have with the persons who care for them when they are so markedly dependent provide the bedrock web of relational fabric from which trust—or mistrust—grows. An abundance of trustworthy encounters between parent and child calls forth a basically trusting approach to other persons. The circle of trust expands as the infant's interactions extend to an ever-increasing number of persons.

The growing capacity to trust other persons becomes a resource for the deepest trust commitments an individual makes in life: trust in God, trust in a spouse, trust in a business partner, and trust in friends. In situations where negative encounters have been predominant, mistrust develops. For these persons the struggle to gain appropriate trust may continue for a lifetime. Early lessons are deep and abiding and can be very difficult to change.

From this very basic, fundamental, initial life stage, we see why family trustworthiness is a requisite if faith is to be nurtured in an optimal climate. A person's capacity to trust in God and in the Christian community has its beginnings in these early life encounters. Beginning in infancy and continuing throughout life, persons strive to achieve a healthy and appropriate balance between trust and mistrust.

Toddler and Preschool Years

Mobility on toddling legs and command over a limited but mushrooming vocabulary open up a whole new world to growing children. They find they have much to learn. They expend boundless energy in conquering their newly discovered world. They keep their little bodies in perpetual motion with brief and sometimes protested stops for food intake and sleeping. They climb up, over, under and into things. They run. They jump. They poke. They crawl. They squirm. They sway. They doddle. If it's new, it's worth exploring. If it's old, it's worth exploring again!

They are superb imitators. They watch parents and often end up doing what parents do. Sometimes these carbon-copy behaviors can be extremely embarrassing to parents who would rather not be reminded of their own life picture quite so vividly. Toddlers watch other children, quickly matching their own behavior to the other child's. They may even go so far as to watch the family pet and try some typical animal movements. They may give new attention to copying some of their favorite characters on television.

The vocabulary of toddlers grows with amazing rapidity. They become more adept at using language structure. Parents no longer have to second guess what the child wants. Bold words and commanding announce "water!" "potty!" "cookie!"

Children are busy gaining a perspective of their own power and independence. Separateness from their mothers, which once seemed scary, now contributes to an expanding sense of self and individuality. "Me do it myself!" are familiar words at this age.

As they move toward ages four and five, children continue in their quest for understanding their world. The questions "Why?" and "How come?" seem to have no end. Sometimes a child asks the question and moves on to another interest before the parent can respond. It is not unusual for the child to ask a question and then lose interest after the first sentence of the parent's response. Some of the questions make no sense from a parental viewpoint. Trying to answer them can be a frustrating challenge.

Respecting the child's exploratory nature is the predominant ingredient of love necessary for faith nurturing at this stage. Allowing the freedom required to move, speak, and question encourages children to believe in their own personhood and to be confident in their own life space. Accepting children's adventurous explorations provides them with open doors for learning. Drawing legitimate limits for children and sensitively encouraging them to establish their own reasonable limits introduces the need to be responsible and accountable. All of these dynamics are part of providing a nurturing climate in which faith can be incorporated into lifelong relational patterns.

Small children are faith pilgrims at the beginning of life's walk. They are running, skipping, and hopping along with eyes and ears wide open to the world of experience—both real and imaginary. Their thinking is devoted to learning and making sense out of life. Their faith issues may be simple, but they are very real. They deserve thoughtful and careful attention.

Elementary School Years

Children continue to grow in independence within their families as they progress through the school years. Their thinking abilities continue to develop as they pursue reading, written expression, and mathematical calculation. With their developing abilities they have the capacity to find answers to many of their questions. They don't have to ask for help from adults as frequently. Their answers are very concrete—which may make them seem overly simplistic to adults—but the important thing to remember is that the answer belongs to the child. As thinking capacities expand, they become (more or less) time managers and have to deal with the consequences of mishandled time.

The relational experiences of school children become increasingly broad. They relate to more people. They have to work their way through a range of experiences—some smooth and easy, others rough and complicated. They soon learn that others don't see the world as they do. They encounter power, injustice, and competitiveness with no parental shield. Although parents may help with analyzing what is happening in situations and lend emotional support, children do much of their relational negotiating on their own. They have much to learn. Things may not turn out as they would like. They deal (usually briefly) with questions like: "What did I do wrong? Where did I mess up? How should I do it next time? Why did my friend get so angry? or Why was my friend (supposedly) so unfair to me?"

In the younger years friendship groups tend to be in a state of flux. The resolution to unsettled relationships is often to join a different group for a while. As children grow older, special friends grow in importance.

If those relationships are to endure, joining another group to escape or avoid an unsettled relationship is not an acceptable answer. There has to be the give and take of genuine negotiation. The players are inexperienced and bungling occurs at frequent intervals. Through the ups and downs much learning takes place. Social patterns are becoming established.

Through their exposure to other people children have opportunities to refine their self-perceptions. They learn that they are gifted in some areas and not so gifted in others. Their bodies and characteristics give one impression while those of their friends give another. Their families do something this way, but the friend down the street comes from a family who doesn't do it at all! Grades in school are often a primary means of comparison; prowess in sports may be another. As they make their comparisons, children begin to build value judgments about themselves leading to ''I'm okay'' or ''I'm not okay'' conclusions. If children happen to be accumulating negative judgments about their own self-worth, low self-esteem confirms itself and grows deeper.

Faith nurturing may also be done outside the family at this stage. Sunday school, camps, sports teams, friendship groups at school or in the neighborhood, and television personalities all can have a substantial impact. Adults other than parents become alternate authority voices. School teachers, league coaches, and scouting leaders may be idealized. Guiding children into quality group life is important at this stage. It also lays a foundation for choosing quality friends.

A trustworthy home environment where the full range of love factors can be practiced in relative security provides a solid social base for children. Realistic affirmation and support help to build self-images that affirm the uniqueness and giftedness of personhood. Ongoing traditions and articulated beliefs help children shape their own identities both in their families and on their own in other settings.

Youth Years

Some of the most rapid and dramatic changes to occur in a lifetime seem to happen in the adolescent years. It sometimes appears as if all aspects of being a person are in flux.

Thinking capacities are expanding. Self-reflection and use of abstract symbols have introduced new avenues of arriving at meaning. Youth can be more analytical and employ powers of reason more accurately. Reflecting on life's experiences exposes past life patterns and yields new insights.

Social skills are being honed. Great stress is often placed on sexuality. What does it mean to be male or female? What are the implications for relationships with my own sex and with the opposite sex? How do I handle the feelings and drives associated with sexuality?

Youth are to a great extent managing relationships quite apart from parents. They are forming relationships with the guidance counselor, the swimming coach, and the youth leader. Lacking experience in all of these arenas, youth sometimes find themselves frustrated with the complexities of human relationships. Long hours of private conversation with friends are spent trying to gain clarity and to decide what step to take next. From a parental perspective it seems that an incredible amount of time goes into teenage relational dynamics.

Physically, bodies which a few years ago obviously belonged to children are shooting up, filling out, and taking on adult proportions and shapes. Fluctuating hormones are bringing physical changes such as problem complexions and emotional instability. Adolescents experience mood swings from the heights of joy to the depths of depression.

Earning money, driving cars, and making one's own decisions are part of a growing urge to be independent from parents. Identification with peers can be at an all-time high as demonstrated by unspoken but rigorous dress codes, language usage, hair styles, perfumes, and whatever else happens to mark a particular youth generation.

Answering the question ''Who am I?'' consumes hours of time and much energy. The search to find an answer is pervasive and intense.

Faith nurturing for the family that includes a teenager can be problematic. The adolescent can refuse to take part in a family tradition one day but be hypercritical at its omission by other members of the family on another occasion. At one time teenagers will participate cooperatively and even enthusiastically only to be rude and sullen at the next occasion.

At the relational level things can be complicated. Teens need warm and accepting support. They need empathic listeners. They may need hard lines of accountability drawn for them. They also need privacy and space. They need separateness and independence. They need freedom. Trying to provide a trustworthy climate for the teenager and all the other members of a family can be like trying to perform a juggling act with too many balls before you've had any instruction in how to do it.

Although there may be a temptation to close up shop on family faith nurturing during the teen years, it is important to keep working at it. Teenagers are forming value systems and shaping lifestyles. At the very time they are experimenting and seeking independence, they are also taking a hard look at family values that have brought them where they are. They may choose not to be a part of much that goes on in the family, but they may rely on and find security in the fact that it is happening. Having a home base is important.

Individual faith nurturing may grow in importance during these years. Personal prayer and Bible reading may receive considerable attention from a teenager. Some teens seek out religious youth clubs or rallies. In contrast, some seem to shelve religion. Yet others get caught up in cults.

The faith-nurturing walk during the teen years can be precarious. It is rarely easy. It can be scary and have far-reaching consequences.

Young Adult Years

Young adults face some of the most difficult decisions in life: decisions about sexuality, marriage, and other close relationships; lifestyle, values, and money; jobs and higher education; membership in groups and organizations; geographic location and living arrangements; health, diet, exercise, and body care; time management; political identification and involvement; and day-to-day living.

To decide on one thing may mean not to decide on another. Two possible choices may lead in very different directions. Some directions once set are changed only with great difficulty. Sometimes they cannot be changed without suffering consequential pain and hurt.

Often a certain amount of isolation and loneliness accompanies young adulthood. One is no longer caught up in the inner workings of the family of origin. The family may be close geographically, but there is an emotional and functional distance. Sometimes the family of origin lives at a geographic distance. In any case there is a separateness between the life of a young adult and the life of the family.

Friends are important, but they can be here today and gone—or at least redefined—tomorrow. They may move to a new job, a distant living arrangement, a marriage, or new interests. The friendship remains, but presence and availability become more limited.

Groups may lend security, but they may be demanding. There are always the decisions about which and how many groups deserve attention.

Faith nurturing during the young adult years rests with the person. The family may draw them in at particular moments. Family can be a source of dependable love and support, but faith nurturing in young adults is for the most part shaped by the decisions they make for their own lives.

Single young adults may chose to identify with churches who have developed specific ministries addressed to their unique needs. Some may pursue life's meaning as a private matter apart from the community life of the church. They may share their journey with a few close friends. Each young adult makes choices regarding faith shaping. The actual configuration takes place over months or years as one decision follows and builds upon another.

If young adults marry, they face the task of determining what faith nurturing will look like in that long-term relationship. These issues are discussed at length in the next chapter.

Young adults who have experienced qualitative faith nurturing in their families earlier in life have a rich resource from which to draw. The search to shape their own faith is undergirded by important insights gained from early life experience and the assurance of having been loved.

The Growing Older Years

Middle age brings with it the realization (or the avoidance of it) that "I have lived several decades of my life." "I am not getting any younger." "Retirement isn't that far away." "I feel an inner urge to be doing those things that are most important to me." "I want my days to count." "I want to contribute to others in lasting and significant ways." Midlife is another "Who am I?" stage of life.

The midlife issues creep up in the midst of years which in many ways have looked much the same. "The kids are just one year older." "I've chalked up another year of work for the company." "I've got a few gray hairs, a cost-of-living raise and a bonus to account for this year." "Well, we splurged and went to Hawaii for two weeks. That's about it for this year." "My hair is a little grayer and the extra pounds won't come off."

These kinds of humdrum years—even though enjoyable and satis-fying—have a kind of routine about them. Except for a vacation here or there, life today looks much like life yesterday. No one expects dramatic changes tomorrow.

The realization that one's time is limited may come as a small, nagging question or a quiet, inner "aha." These days don't go on forever. The changes are amounting to something. Three extra pounds one year have turned into fifteen pounds in five years; and they stick like glue. The realization may be triggered by an unexpected, shocking event. The doctor diagnoses adult-onset diabetes; a best friend the same age suffers a stroke; a grandchild is born. However it comes, the realization stands out in **boldface.** There's a limited amount of time and you want it to count.

Often this kind of midlife realization comes when persons are carrying heavy loads in their jobs, in family involvements with parents and with children, in community responsibilities, and in making personal goals and dreams come true.

Midlife is another period for facing weighty decisions in response to the question: "What changes do I need and want to make so that my life counts?"

The answers midlife persons arrive at are uniquely their own. What these solutions look like depends a great deal on how they have lived, the negotiable and nonnegotiable aspects of their lives, the degree to which the way they are living corresponds to deeply held values, their relational involvements and support structures, their openness to face the issues in depth, the amount of resistance to change, and the extent of their personal energy.

Faith may take on new dimensions in midlife. A number of avenues lie within the realm of possibility. We'll consider a few brief examples.

A father senses that he has talked a great deal about loving his wife and kids, but he has been unavailable to them in presence and time. He changes his schedule. His behavior begins to match his words.

A mother who had literally walked away from her marriage and three children in her midthirties reconnects with the children. She feels she has to handle the situation now rather than continue to postpone it.

A man who has been very active in the church and in service projects in the community backs away to spend time in study and reflection. A woman who has been diligent about prayer and study decides it is time for her to engage in some kind of meaningful, worthwhile action.

A woman who has left her musical talent largely unused develops it and offers it to the church. Her friend who has consistently used her musical gifts decides to go back to school to study counseling. She drops her musical involvements in the church to provide study time.

A doctor rearranges his schedule to attend worship regularly by limiting his on-call duty to once a month.

A lawyer resigns her lucrative position in corporate law to accept a lesser salary working in behalf of welfare clients who can't afford standard legal fees.

The middle years gradually blend into the senior years of life. There is no one age when these growing older stages arrive. For a period one feels confident that one is not in the senior years, and then comes a day when one knows the stage has at least begun.

In the senior years the body slows down. The struggle to maintain health may be continuous. A good day is relative. Hair, if uncolored, is mostly gray, silver, white, or missing. Mental processes may be slower. Retirement has come and gone, replaced by other ways of structuring life.

Social relationships change. Some friends and relationships die. Some have moved to warmer climates, to retirement villages, to be close to grown children, to smaller homes.

Time looks different now. The younger generation seems to be frenzied and stressed. Young people are constantly on the move with no appreciation for time spent in reflection—or in just sitting.

There is an inevitable facing of one's own death and the death of others. A certain kind of readiness develops, creating a freedom to live each day exactly as you choose.

Faith nurturing of senior adults is usually less learning new truths than it is embracing old ones. The thoughts may go something like this:

"My life wasn't all that I hoped it would be, but I was faithful in a lot of things and God was good to me."

"Given a serious illness it is by God's love that I have one more day to live. It could be the last."

"I did some awful things in my life, but I can't change that. God's grace covers it all."

"Going to be with God won't be bad at all. I've lived a lot of years here. I've met many people and seen a lot of things. I dread being cooped up in a nursing home. When God is ready, I'm ready."

It is not that senior adults spend considerable time brooding over impending death. It is more a matter of readiness; when the end of life on this earth comes, they are ready.

For senior adults who have nurtured faith through the years, the life tasks of dealing with decreasing energy and health, retiring from work, making meaningful contributions, facing death, and planning for care may seem overwhelming, but there is an assurance of God's sustaining love and grace. They have walked through good and bad times and have known God's presence. God will continue to be a very present help regardless of what tomorrow brings.

There may be some older adults who have not nurtured a faith in

God through the years. They have had other life priorities. However, in the final life stages they may become open to God's love for them. They may decide to develop their faith even at this late hour.

Life's Crises

The normal development of life with all of its stages and tasks may be shaped very differently in the event of a severe, unpredicted, life-changing crisis. Timing is always bad for a crisis. There is no readiness—it just hits. Available resources are taxed to the limit. Life may seem to lose all meaning, at least for a period of time.

Profound questions inevitably accompany a crisis.

What is going on? Why?

Why does it have to be me?

Did I do something wrong?

Can't I just die and not go on?

How can I possibly get through this?

Where is God?

Why isn't God stopping all of this?

Crises bring a web of hurtful circumstances. There is no direction to move in without feeling pain. In the midst of a crisis there is no way to escape facing meaningful issues. What is God's place in all of this? If God is near, then God must be very angry or very punitive to let this happen. If God is distant, then the individual is left alone in despair. These are hard issues to resolve.

Perspective on life is usually very mixed in the midst of crisis. Ambiguities and uncertainties abound. Faith answers, which in better times seemed adequate, no longer suffice. More adequate answers seem illusive. At the same time the presence and love of God is real and sustaining. Trust is deepened. In the midst of uncertainties God gives each day a purpose.

Crises bring intense needs for faith nurturing. It may be less a matter of doing traditional things or relating verbal assurances than simply being present—one faith person alongside another symbolizing and experiencing something of God's love.

The Place of Individual Development in Family Faith Nurturing

Families are composed of individual members bound together in relationships. Understanding what is happening in the personal lives of its members helps the entire family to be sensitive to a number of factors related to qualitative faith nurturing.

The balance between individual and total family approaches to faith nurturing can be adjusted in light of individual stages. The most pertinent issues can be addressed. The most effective ways and methods can be selected. The boundaries and degrees of participation can be redefined. The most relevant dimensions of love can be emphasized.

To ignore individual developmental stages is to weaken the quality of faith nurturing in the family. Another developmental aspect which interacts with the impact of faith nurturing is the developmental stage of the family unit itself. Many of the issues raised in this chapter will be expanded as we consider the interactions between individual development, family development, and qualitative faith nurturing in chapter 7.

Questions for Reflection and Discussion

1. What life stages are represented in your family?

2. What faith issues seem to be facing family members because of their life stages?

3. How have you recycled the issues of a previous life stage? What difference did a new perspective make?

4. How have life crises interacted with your faith development?

7

❧❧❧

Faith Nurturing and the Cycle of Family Life

The Christian faith from its earliest roots has been expressed through a community of believing persons—God's people. While there is unquestionably a personal dimension to being a Christian, it is in becoming a part of the community of believers that the individual Christian experiences the power, the joy, and the challenge of the faith. The Holy Spirit was given to the body of believers; the written Word was entrusted to the faith community. Christians find their fullest identity in the context of fellow believers with whom they join in worship, sing praises, pray, and engage in service.

Considering faith nurturing of individuals provides a crucial perspective, but a holistic viewpoint would also include nurturing of the faith community as a body—a group of believers committed to enriching and deepening their life together. The focus of this chapter, then, is on nurturing the family as a microcommunity of faith from the time it begins through its various stages of development.

Early studies of family life were based on developmental stages.[1] Families have a moment of birth and progress through a series of stages.

Developing adequate models for describing the various stages of family life has been a formidable challenge. The work continues today. Those who concentrate their study in this area continue to affirm the validity of the developmental perspective as crucial to understanding how families function and operate. The formulation of adequate models is complicated, but recent contributions demonstrate that there has been progress in addressing the relevant issues.[2]

In light of newly emerging insights into family development we

107

would be remiss not to include a chapter pointing to some of the implications of developmental stages in families for faith nurturing. An approach to faith nurturing which seems to be a perfect fit for an early stage when a family is just beginning may be abandoned at a later stage because the once perfect fit no longer exists.

We will briefly describe the general stages and highlight some of the faith-nurturing issues related to each stage. Given that we are being selective regarding the issues, you may think of others which could have been included with a particular stage.

The Early Stages

Engagement

When a woman and a man begin to sense that there is a significance and a depth to their togetherness that is leading them to a long-range relationship, they usually decide to become engaged.

Engaged couples operate with what has been called a "romantic halo" which each places over the other and their relationship. The halo denotes the extreme idealization of the other person and what that means for the relationship. The other is seen as being nearly perfect. Weaknesses are denied, ignored, or minimized. Sexual attraction is high. Any information from outside sources that challenges these ideal illusions is usually unheard or at least unattended to. Adoring eyes meet in prolonged encounters that communicate "We were meant for each other. Our relationship is the best that anyone could ever have. It will endure this way forever."

One faith-nurturing issue to be faced during engagement is whether the individuals have initially explored who each is as a faith person and how that will influence who they are as a couple. Many times the cherished illusions each person holds about the other are characterized by the exclusion of entire life arenas.

We (Myron and Jan) discovered during the course of our premarital counseling that we had hardly touched on the subject of political parties. It wasn't an easy topic for us. Jan's parents were active in one party; Myron's, in the other. To which party would each of us belong? Some couples exclude faith and religious identity from discussions of their future. Such exclusion does not mean these areas are unimportant; indeed, they can become fertile ground for conflict in the marriage.

A second issue involves negotiating how the couple will relate to the faith commitments each has made earlier. Such negotiation was often unnecessary in previous historical periods when prescribed roles informed husbands and wives who they were to each other and what their marriage meant for their identity. Given the change in prescribed roles today and the raised consciousness that male and female were created equally precious before God, answers that might have sufficed in previous years may be rejected today.

One of our students spoke proudly of his wife who had achieved specialized scientific research training and was engaged in a significant project at the time. They were living in the area because of her work. He explained that prior to their marriage they had spent long hours in conversation about their life together. She was entering a graduate science program which accepted only the most talented students. It was an honor to be selected. He was a liberal arts major in college with broad interests. "It just made sense to go where her gifts could be used. . . . I'm just glad we agreed on it before we got married. It was part of the bargain."

The third issue for faith nurturing for the engaged couple involves the challenge of incarnating the dimensions of God's love into the couple's ways of relating prior to the wedding. Because the message "I love you" is sent so regularly both verbally and nonverbally during this period, testing the trustworthiness of that love is rarely done. Two examples show the importance of addressing the steadfastness of human love, even in the early days of a relationship.

A young couple was planning their wedding. The blueprint kept becoming more elaborate and more costly. Neither family had large sums of money. The expenditures soon approached an astronomical level in light of the family resources. The young man grew skeptical and alienated. He withdrew from the process of further wedding plans but gave his young bride no other signs of his discomfort. The wedding was a grand affair.

Over a decade later this couple sat with a counselor to discover if they had a future together. She asked her husband, "When did you start becoming so angry with me?" She was shocked when he went back as far as their wedding plans. "But you didn't say anything that I remember. Why not?" she probed.

"I was afraid you wouldn't understand where I was coming from," he said. "You were pretty high on having your own way then, just like you are now. I thought I would lose you. Back then I couldn't face that possibility. Today it's different."

She was furious; he withdrew. Within several months they decided to get a divorce. They had avoided testing the quality of their love. The love struggles between them had affected their lives through the years. Their energies continually went into the battles between them. There was little left for personal growth, caring for children, or faithfulness to God.

Another couple tested their love directly. She became anxious when he presented her with an engagement ring. She knew there were critical things she had not told him from her past. As a teenager she had given birth to a son out of wedlock and placed him for adoption. She spent weeks deliberating whether or not she should tell this to her future husband. Finally she decided she simply could not keep that secret from him if they were to live trustworthy lives together. She told her story. He was stunned and hurt. It took awhile, but later he affirmed both God's forgiveness and also his own. They agreed it would not be a wall or a weapon between them. They were married knowing that in light of God's forgiveness their love could forgive and move on.

Early Marriage

The early years of marriage, particular for young couples, are filled with life-determining decisions, establishing long-lasting relational patterns and shaping their lives together.

Newly married couples are confronted with many decisions which set their direction for years to come. How to get and spend money, where to live geographically, how to obtain housing, what roles each will have, whether or not and when to have children, and what groups to participate in are all important decisions. Some of the decisions lead to directions in life which are very difficult, if not impossible to change later.

In the early years of marriage relational patterns are formed. These patterns may not be talked about, but they emerge as the couple go about the business of daily living. They become almost like a computer program which performs in a certain way every time it is put into motion. All kinds of life arenas are guided and regulated by these patterns. Power distribution, methods of expressing affirmation, ways of managing conflict, frequency and methods of sexual union, communication networks, and negotiation procedures are all firmly established.

The shape of togetherness unique to that couple is determined over time. "This is *us*." "This is *he*." "This is *she*." These issues are gradually worked out.

Role distribution is one area where many conflicts ensue in early marriage. Who will do what? When? Where? Why? How? For how long? An incredibly small task may lead to a prolonged and sometimes heated discussion concerning these questions. As a husband and wife work at shaping their identity as a couple, they are also continuing to define their individual personhoods within the context of marriage.

A faith-nurturing issue that stands out in these early years will be the decisions made in answer to the questions: How important is personal and shared faith in this marriage? How will it be shaped? What will we share? What will her faith be like? What will his faith be like? Because there are a number of momentous decisions to be made during this period, there may be a tendency to see faith as just another thing to work on. It may even be placed on a back burner.

It is our conviction that shaping a couple's faith identity is primary. His faith, her faith, and their shared faith can then serve as a basis from which other decisions can be made.

Shaping a shared faith identity may not be easy. We (Jan and Myron) struggled. Perhaps because our faith similarities had drawn us together, we expected shared faith to be simple. Not so! When it came to daily devotions, we found that Myron did it one way with his set of expectations. Jan's ways and expectations were very different. We tried a number of approaches. Inevitably one of us felt frustrated. After several years of struggle we decided that perhaps that particular faith area would be best handled separately. We would share some things together during special seasons of the church year or during crises when we needed this kind of togetherness in special ways. These would be above and beyond our personal disciplines.

Another faith issue revolves around a couple's conscious commitment to devote time, thought, and energy working at becoming more Christ-like. Such a commitment involves reflection on the quality of love and trustworthiness shown in their relational patterns, negotiation as to how they could do better, and conscious devotion of energy to that improvement. The quality of marital relationship would inevitably be enhanced if couples were to concentrate on trustworthy caring and responding, accountability, giving and receiving, knowing and respecting, and forgiveness.

We left a wedding one day completely frustrated, with each of us experiencing feelings of discomfort. As we talked about it, we zeroed in on the source of our feelings. Most of the emphasis of that wedding had been on the two persons as individuals and their intent to leave each other free to be themselves. The togetherness thread went something like this: "We will walk side by side and live together. If the other needs help in the walk toward personal goals, I will try to be there for that person." It took only a few years for that marriage to disintegrate. We question whether they ever really knew each other.

A third faith issue faced by early marrieds involves coming to terms with their differing religious backgrounds in terms of tradition and practices. During the romantic halo period such differences are likely to have been minimized. After the wedding they must face reality. In some marriages many questions may have to be addressed; in others, few. Some typical questions are: To what denomination will we belong? How active will we be? How much support will we give in terms of money and involvement?

Prior to his marriage one young man had given money generously to his church. His wife objected. She came from a family who lived on a restricted budget. It took them months to find a mutually satisfactory answer.

Some of the most consequential decisions couples make are those surrounding the question of whether or not to have children. When children enter a family there is a fundamental change in the nature of that family system. Early developmental models of families were built totally on the theory that all couples had children. More recent models attempt to indicate the tremendous significance of this particular decision. Family life for couples with children looks very different from family life for couples who have no children. Faith-nurturing issues faced by these two kinds of families are distinctive.

Couples without Children

Compared to earlier generations, couples today have many options related to child bearing. Many factors contribute to the decision about whether or not to have children. Today more couples are choosing not to have them. Many reasons could be listed. However, Christian couples should not base the decision primarily on convenience, expediency, or self-gratification. Rather, it should be firmly based on solid theological grounds.

Couples who are not committed to raising children have numerous resources available to them which parents simply don't have—at least during the most active parenting years. The primary faith issue facing these Christian couples is ministry and service. The resources these couples have can be used in many ways. Seeking God's will becomes a central task for use of time, money, energy, and personal gifts.

Couples with Children

Children are time- and energy-consuming persons. The extent of personal investment which must be made by parents may come as a shock when the first infant enters the family.

A young mother being interviewed on a television talk show confessed that in no way had she anticipated the kind of time it would take to care for the tiny infant in her arms. We chuckled, remembering our own amazement. How can an entire day go by and the baby's care consume nearly the whole time?

We believe that children are gifts from God, given to parents for responsible nurturing until they reach independent adulthood. Parents are God's stewards when it comes to nurturing children.

There are great rewards in parenting. There are also considerable costs and investments to be made. Moments of joy come as serendipitous gifts. Deep and lasting pain may also intrude on the parenting walk. All of the parents we have met attest to their experience that nurturing children has its ups and downs.

Faith nurturing in families with young children needs to be multi-leveled. Children require nurturing appropriate to their life stage. To a great extent this task has been entrusted to the parents. In trying to meet this challenge parents may lose sight of their own needs to continue being nurtured. As other children enter the family, more levels of faith nurturing are introduced. The task is complex!

There seem to be no easy answers as to how to do it well. Expectations and goals need to be realistic given the demands of family living. Much of faith nurturing in families with young children may center around love and trust-building skills in relationships. While not always overtly recognized as deeply religious, these lie at the core of establishing a faith-nurturing climate.

Traditional spiritual disciplines practiced by parents may become very difficult to execute. At a conference on spiritual life a middle-aged man offered a suggestion to other conferees about his approach to cultivating a relationship with God. His answer had been to have daily Bible reading and prayer time at a specific hour each day. He expounded his story. For over twenty years he had set aside thirty minutes from 6:30 to 7 A.M. He has missed only two or three times because of extraordinary circumstances.

The next day in a workshop Jan was leading there was an emotional reaction to this man's testimony from women who had raised or were in the process of raising children. They were joined by some young fathers in the group. There was no way they could count on 6:30 to 7 A.M. every day being available for personal devotions. Most of them struggled to find personal time at all. One of them confessed that after attending to the needs of the children all day and tucking them into bed at night, "I'm literally exhausted. If I do much of anything, it's to watch an hour or so of television."

One woman whose children were now in high school or college reported that in the last few years she had recaptured what having regular daily quiet time meant. "I was lucky to breathe a prayer here or there during the day when the kids were all living at home. I felt guilty about that for so long. Then I decided maybe raising the kids in a reasonably happy and loving home was a form of prayer for me. I felt better then." Reflecting on her comment the whole group sat for a moment in silence.

Single Parents

The number of single parents is growing. A careful analysis of their specific situation lies beyond the space parameters of this volume. We want to note, however, that we are aware of many of the pressures faced in these situations. The relational developmental cycle experienced by couples has been truncated. Resources have been sharply cut. In many situations survival with a reasonable degree of happiness becomes the goal.

There is a need for faith nurturing in these families as in any other family. Yet the need may be much more demanding. Time is at a premium. Energies are spent doing the tasks that have to be done. We have heard single parents talk about the constant feeling of getting further and further behind on nearly every level of their lives.

Many single parents have reported that they have not found the church to be very accepting or supportive of their situation. Church schedules and programming can add to the burden of life rather than help lift it.

Some congregations have developed a specialized ministry to single parents. These have often mushroomed in attendance, attesting to the fact that the needs are there. The unique needs must be addressed in relevant ways and through structures that fit the demanding schedules and responsibilities of single parents.

In summary, establishing patterns for faith nurturing during the early stages of marriage does much to set the tone for later years. To be effective the patterns must fit the relational needs and structure of the family. The challenge of faith nurturing is great. Trying to meet the challenge can be exhilarating, yet also very taxing.

The Later Stages

The Middle Years

It would take a carefully constructed collage with many pictures to create an image which communicates all the forms marriage and family living can take in the middle-year stages.

Many couples are entering the empty-nest phase, having finally launched their last child from the home. Others, by choice or not by choice, are having that last baby. Some empty nesters are adjusting to having their young adult children move back home to conserve money and gain support! Mothers are going back to school or entering the work force. Fathers may be seeking a job change, having burned out on twenty years or more of doing the same tasks and withstanding the same old pressures. Couples without children sense a need for change. Singles may be trying marriage again or for the first time. Couples may be living separately by choice or because of extenuating circumstances. Aging parents may have joined the family unit. If you think of the middle-years families you know, you can create a collage of your own with real faces and concrete situations.

Some of the tasks faced in middle-years relationships, however they may be shaped, include coming to terms with personal midlife emotional and physical agendas, assuming responsibility for care of aged parents, shaping time and energy priorities so that life counts, accepting younger adults as peers, welcoming grandchildren into the world, following through on earlier "We'll-do-it-later" dreams (or exchanging old dreams for new ones), and preparing for the senior years.

It is in the context of these weighty life tasks that faith nurturing is done. We want to lift up three issues of faith nurturing that seem most common in these years.

Within individuals there is often an intense urgency to discover and devote energy to that which makes life meaningful for the individual. The relational implications of this drive can take many forms. In some marriages couples experience more intimacy than ever before. The quest for deeper life meaning has brought them to very similar places. Now they are ready to link arms and press forward together.

In contrast, other couples may find that there seems to be increased distance mounting between them. They are going different ways uniquely their own. They need permission to pursue the directions life is pulling. In this situation it becomes a matter of allowing each other space in which to think and move.

Pursuing who you need and want to be is a consuming task. This need may appear slowly like a growing flower. It may also present itself rather suddenly as if out of nowhere.

Midlife issues have to do with faith. What counts? What has meaning? What takes priority? What has deep and abiding value? One person's answers may not seem religious from another person's point of view. The consuming nature of the quest may cause one person to feel neglected by the other.

Myron's dad was a fascinating midlifer whose life agendas influenced the entire family. He ran his own small business selling, installing, and repairing radios and televisions. In his late thirties he began to read commentaries and other religious books which would illuminate more clearly the Bible's message for him. Through his forties we watched him study for hours. The whole family supported his efforts and was proud of his achievements. He became one of the most biblically astute laymen we have ever known. Being prepared each week to teach his adult Sunday school class became a central goal. He didn't talk about his learnings at any great length or depth. He worked some of them into his teaching. Many seemed to be important simply because they had helped him grow in his own understanding. That was sufficient. He didn't need to share them. In the meantime he put aside previous interests, such as the family boat.

Today we have a number of Dad Chartier's books in our library. In many ways their primary importance to us lies in the memory of the person who spent hours avidly gleaning their content to expand his understanding of the biblical message. Dad modeled something very special about pursuing midlife's quest for meaning in the midst of heavy family and business responsibilities. The picture lesson for us has been indelible.

Some persons withdraw and recoil from the inner search for meaning. They may immerse themselves in fast-lane, on-the-surface living which keeps them going at a frenetic pace but provides little depth. Eventually this approach wears thin and the more basic tasks of midlife have to be addressed with integrity and depth.

Another faith issue which is often faced during midlife is related to making one's life count for others in a broad sense. Earlier years may have been spent making life energies count for a person and his family, but midlifers often see a wider vision.

In a marriage midlife couples may have over fifty years of accumulated relational experience between them. They have been through many life experiences. Although they may not have given conscious time to serious reflection, they have undoubtedly learned some crucial lessons. Where does all of this life experience go? How does it get invested where it counts?

Finding outlets for expression of the need to serve and to give is another faith agenda. It has to do with giftedness.

In this area, too, couples can become more intimate or experience the need for space to develop in ways apart from each other. A faith challenge is to find outlets that contribute to the well-being and wholeness of humanity rather than to increased alienation and brokenness.

A family tension which frequently arises is that while midlife parents are feeling the need to pass on their life wisdom to younger generations, their adolescent or young adult children are trying to break away and arrive at their own values and lifestyles independent of parents.

These may not be easy years for family living. We believe the tensions are best handled when they are talked about and negotiated in a context of love and trust.

A third faith issue for midlifers is being confronted with human mortality—one's own and others. For some persons this confrontation has happened much earlier, but midlifers seemingly can't escape it. It is generally unsettling at the innermost levels.

Myron's mother was forty-seven when Dad Chartier died. In the six previous years her four children had left home to pursue their own lives. She had a new home in the country which represented a shared dream come true, but the one she had lived to share it with was dead.

We lived at a distance. For a number of years Mom's letters raised questions: "What is God doing in all of this? What difference can my life make now? Why doesn't God take my life away, too?" On occasion she shared some of her thoughts: "If I had known Dad would die so young, I might have. . . . If only the Lord would come, then I would be able to. . . . If I would have died first. . . . If the children lived closer. . . ."

Mom's walk taught us much about how heavy and weighty the midlife years can be. Her questions and her thoughts were real and deep. One cannot respond to issues related to death with easy, simple, or ready answers.

Humans don't live forever. We can live for years, and everything seems to go on as usual. Then death claims someone who has been very special. It may even be someone younger than ourselves. A hole, a vacuum results. Life isn't going on in the same way anymore. The death of another person raises core issues about one's life and one's own death. What does my life mean? When and how will it end? What lies beyond? How much of a hole will be left when I die? How will my loved ones face my death and go on?

The faith-nurturing issues of midlife are penetratingly deep. They elude definitive answers. They seem to require ongoing attention as life moves through its cycles.

The Senior Years

The relational years which come with advancing age have their rewards and joys, pains and frustrations. The tasks of senior adulthood include dealing with decreased energy and capacity, coping with physical disability as it comes, loss of close friends and relatives through death, facing one's own death, contributing to younger generations, and communicating one's accumulated wisdom to others in some fashion.

As long as one's health remains good, the senior years can be ones wherein persons make their most significant, long-lasting contributions to others. They can be years for doing many of the postponed things.

Time becomes more precious but less frenetic. One has time for reflection, reading, watching television, sitting quietly, talking, or walking leisurely. Many things in life don't have to be done today; they can wait for tomorrow or next week.

We (Myron and Jan) have been blessed by senior adult family and friends who have modeled for us pictures of the productiveness, enjoyment, and joyousness that can predominate old age with all of its frustrations and perplexities.

Such persons have contributed to our lives in significant ways. The life portraits they have created for us have a wholeness and a completeness often lacking in the fast-paced sketches presented by younger persons. We would like to point to faith issues which have been presented to us by these persons as being particularly significant.

First, it is important to use some of the available time to focus on the presence of God. It involves allowing one's inner self to be open to becoming more Christlike.

David and Vera Mace invited a group of us attending a marriage enrichment event to join them in an abbreviated form of their daily quiet/sharing time. We were to spend the first few minutes in quiet prayer and reflection. At the appropriate moment we were to turn to one another and share from our quiet experience. To give a focus David read a verse of Scripture before we began. We sat in silence for five minutes.

David and Vera modeled their sharing before the group. They talked softly of many things. They spoke of the poverty they had seen in so many parts of the world and their comparatively feeble attempts to live simply. They mentioned David's health and Vera's tendency to worry about it. Vera told of her gratefulness for God's goodness in giving them these beautiful years together. David's eyes twinkled as he listened. "I had almost the same thoughts," he said.

Our eyes were teary as we listened to this most intimate sharing. Jan was reminded of an elderly aunt and uncle who read daily from a portion of the Gospels and talked about applying it to their lives—a shared practice which they began in their senior years.

A second faith issue is learning to rely on God's presence and undergirding strength through all of life's experiences—including death. Facing pain and suffering is extremely difficult. It may be most difficult to witness if one's spouse is the one experiencing severe pain. There is often little one can do except to be present.

The possibility of death that seemed remote in younger years is an ever-present reality for senior adults. Today they are together in their marriage; tomorrow one of them may be gone. Which one? When and how will it happen? How will the one who is left live? These are hard questions. Answers come only through living.

Jan's dad was convinced he would die before his wife. In his mid-seventies he spent time getting things prepared to assure that Mom Duncan would be well cared for. He was absolutely certain of the order of events. He refused to consider any other possibility. Statistics said he would die first. Two of his brothers had already died of strokes, leaving their wives to cope as widows. Actually he outlived Mom by one year!

There is much uncertainty about tomorrow. Today a couple can manage their house. Tonight one of them may fall, and tomorrow they will have to face the possibility of moving to a one-level apartment.

Trusting in God's grace and goodness becomes crucial during these years. Such trust often involves giving up some of the control and self-reliance of earlier years. Accepting the support ministries of younger generations can be a tremendous blessing.

Letting go and entrusting one's own care or the care of one's spouse to others is a part of this faith issue. Over the last few years we have watched an older couple deal with letting go and death. One winter the wife became very ill. Her mind and body were affected. Her husband cared for her with great devotion. We often stopped to say ''hello'' as we walked in the evenings. Two summers passed. Her condition gradually deteriorated. The next spring he was sitting on the porch alone. We inquired about his wife.

Tears slowly trickled down his cheeks as he told the story. ''She got so bad. I had to put her in a nursing home. I was sick myself this winter. I just couldn't take care of her anymore. She doesn't even recognize me. She just lies there and stares.'' He paused awhile and added, ''God's going to have to take care of us from here on in. I've done the best I could.'' His wife died the next winter.

For a couple of years he kept the house tidy and yard neatly trimmed. Last winter we noticed one week that there were no lights on in his house. In the summer the house went up for sale. A new family moved in. Their faith in God had sustained that old couple all the way through.

A third faith issue concerns embracing the afterlife as a certain and healing opportunity. The afterlife can be viewed as a rather dubious blessing when life is active and rewarding. If one has to die, it is nice to know there is a life beyond this one, but there is nothing particularly attractive about this alternative *now*.

When friends and family members have died, when one's body is full of pain, one's perspective may change. Somewhere, sometime the point comes when death followed by life with God becomes a true blessing. Time, then, becomes waiting for the end—and the new beginning.

A close friend died two years ago after more than a decade of battling cancer. She lived a full and active life through it all. She required concentrated care during only the last few weeks. In January her health became more problematic. In February she was experiencing constant pain. She still talked about fighting for life. ''I'm not giving up yet,'' she told Jan on the phone. ''I'm waiting for the new baby (a grandchild due the end of April). I want to be at a wedding anniversary celebration this summer. Then I'll see!'' When Jan talked with her two weeks later, her condition had worsened. ''I'm not sure about all of this,'' she confessed as she described her condition. ''I don't want to be a burden. I'd rather go soon.''

Two weeks later we talked with her for the last time. She had weakened considerably. Her voice was frail; her speech was slow. She talked of being grateful for the care her family was giving her. She was thankful for the ministry of the hospice. Her elderly mother had come to visit. She could see friends for only short periods. "I'm ready to go! Whatever life with God is like, it's got to be better than this," she whispered.

With a bit of her typical humor she added with a chuckle, "The baby will come whether I'm here or not."

Myron sat down after that phone call and wrote her a letter. Some lines went like this:

.... We as God's people live in the light of the resurrection hope. As death brings a dark night between us, God in his own time will bring the dawn of eternity. When death ends your life here, I live for that time in God's eternity when we will be able to say to each other:

"Good morning, Ardelle."
"Good morning, Myron."
Until then God's grace and peace will sustain us.
I love you, Ardelle.
    Myron

When the family called to tell us of her death, they said that she had asked for that letter to be read several times the last few days of her life. The "good morning" lines were incorporated in the funeral sermon.

Our friend's faith was strong. Her faith undergirded her walk into death. Life with God had for her become the preferred alternative. She had come to the point where she was ready to die. She could choose and affirm death.

Someday we will meet her again. Someday she will meet the grandson who was born the day after she died and the new child who joined the family this year.

We have not been comprehensive in discussing the faith issues related to developmental stages of family life. This chapter could be expanded to make an entire book. If we left unsaid things you believe ought to have been articulated, accept our attempt as basic and guiding. Move beyond it with your own experience and stories. There is much yet to be explored and written on nurturing faith throughout the family life cycle.

Questions for Reflection and Discussion

1. Are you able to identify the development of your family from its beginning? Could you make a line drawing of major decisions and events in your family from its beginning to the present?

2. How do you see couple faith identity in your family? How does it compare with individual faith identity?

3. Do you agree with the authors that whether or not a couple has children makes a significant difference in the shape of family faith nurturing? What illustrations can you give to support your opinion?

4. What are some of the costs and rewards you have experienced in parenting? How has faith nurturing interacted with those costs and rewards?

5. What did the authors leave unsaid in this chapter that seems important for you to add?

PART FOUR
The Ways of Faith Nurturing in the Family

8

Finding Your Way in Family Faith Nurturing

Nurturing the faith of a family is something like being an artist who paints breathtaking landscapes with oils of many hues. Part of the painting is done with broad strokes that sweep across the canvas. When the broad strokes are complete enough to create the desired effect, the artist works with small brushes to add the detail. The vagueness of the broad strokes comes alive with trees, a lake, two fishermen in a boat, a family enjoying a picnic lunch, and horses grazing in the meadow.

Family faith nurturing has dimensions that are very much like the broad strokes and the fine strokes employed by the artist. In chapter 1 we referred to Deuteronomy 6:4-9. This passage implies the broad strokes of faith nurturing done by demonstrating one's love for God through all of the relationships of family living. It also mentions some concrete methods used as fine strokes to create the specific content and detail. In this final chapter we will discuss the broad strokes of family faith nurturing, the necessity of each family finding its own way, and finally the fine strokes which consist of specific method and content.

The Broad Strokes of Family Faith Nurturing
Love and Trust

In family faith nurturing, creating a climate of trustworthy love is like the broad strokes of the artist. The importance of that relational climate where love, integrity, and trustworthiness are givens can hardly be overemphasized.

In the context of love and trust persons are set free to take the risks that will move them toward wholeness. The climate invites them to grow. It undergirds the growth process with acceptance and affirmation.

On the other hand, to the extent that a relational climate is unloving and untrustworthy faith growth is blocked. It becomes stunted. It may even deteriorate.

Families may spend considerable time doing specific faith-nurturing methods together. They may use some qualitative curriculum resources. These are noteworthy endeavors, but their effectiveness may be minimal because there is little trust, and love in that family is conditional and manipulative. Sometimes children raised in these kinds of environments rebel against the family faith. They come to believe that the faith which was talked about was the primary cause of lack of love and trust among family members.

We believe there is a lack of congruence between the Christian faith and relational environments in which persons act in unloving, untrustworthy ways with one another. In relational contexts where love and trust are clearly present, the Christian faith finds a congruent environment in which it can be lived out.

Part 2 of this book was written to help clarify the meaning of love and trust as well as to point to the implications for relational living in the family. Without these broad strokes attempts at faith nurturing may produce minimal or even negative outcomes. Living in loving, trustworthy relationships provides the environment where the qualities of the Christian faith are experienced in day-to-day living. Growth thrives in this kind of congruent climate. The challenge is to establish such a climate.

Modeling and Mirroring

Two educational approaches, modeling and mirroring, seem to have particular relevance for creating a broad-stroke nurturing environment characterized by love and trust.[1] Both of these approaches do less to teach in a direct manner than to set the tone in which love, trust, and faith slowly emerge in the context of family relationships.

Modeling. Jesus modeled through both his words and his actions. The meanings of his words were lived out in his behavior. On occasion he interpreted his behavior through his words. Jesus was a living portrait of God's love. He showed us the way of faith and spoke to us about its meaning. Jesus was a model of faith.

In family faith nurturing we are to be faith models to one another. We are to speak of and show the ways of being the best faith persons that we can be. Of course, a primary implication is that we are to give our best to live in trustworthy, caring relationships. Parents, in particular, are called to a modeling approach in which their telling and speaking come together in coherent ways with their doing. Modeling is not restricted to the parental role. Husbands and wives can be models to each other. Children in their developing faith walk may become models for one another, for their parents, and for members of their extended family.

One caution needs to be raised with regard to modeling. Sometimes modeling is interpreted as if one has to be perfect to be a model. This is not so. Modeling requires that we present our own story, our own struggles, and our own learnings in being faithful pilgrims. To present ourselves as perfect serves primarily to convince others that we are neither realistic nor trustworthy!

Mirroring. Jesus was a "mirror" to the persons among whom he lived. Through his words and deeds he not only interpreted who he was, but he also reflected back to the people who they were as faith persons. Jesus was a mirror to the woman at the well when he spoke to her of her five husbands. He was a mirror to the people who were about to stone the woman caught in adultery when he suggested that the person without sin be the first to cast a stone. Jesus mirrored both the faithfulness and the sinfulness of humankind back to those with whom he related.

In family faith nurturing mirroring is an important dynamic. Through mirroring persons receive feedback as to how they are progressing with their faith walk. The images that human beings hold of themselves are usually very biased and incomplete. They need observations from others regarding their behavior to fill out and correct the distorted self-pictures they have created.

Mirroring should include a healthy balance of positive and negative elements. The emphasis should be on the positive. Faith pilgrims need to be affirmed when their walk has been faithful. However, pilgrims also need to know when they have missed the mark in one way or another. A helpful mirroring approach will not only point out the person's mistakes and shortcomings, but also suggest ways for improvement whenever possible.

Mirroring has often been ineffective because it has focused almost exclusively on the negative. Little or no attention has been given to tell others what they have done well. Effective mirroring works to achieve a balance of the two.

Sensitivity is a requirement for qualitative modeling and mirroring.

These two educational approaches can be effective in helping establish a favorable climate for faith nurturing if sensitively implemented into the give and take of family relationships.

Finding Your Way as a Family

How your family will nurture its members in the faith will be unique. That uniqueness applies to both the broad strokes and the fine strokes of painting your family's picture of faith.

There is no one way or correct way to nurture your family members in a trusting relationship with God. How your family goes about painting the broad strokes of trustworthy love and modeling and mirroring will look different from the way other families go about the same task. How your family paints the fine strokes of faith content and method will vary also from other families.

Why is this so? Each family is different from every other family. Families are like fingerprints. No two sets are alike. Families are like cultures; no two appear the same. There may be similarities, but there are no identical twins.

How are families different? With a little thought you could quickly come up with your own list. Allow us to name a few ways in which families differ. First, families differ in composition. In some families there may be one parent (father) and one child (female). In another there may be one parent (mother) and two children (male and female). In yet another there may be no parents, just children; the older ones caring for the younger ones. In still another family there may be a father, mother, brother, adopted sister, and grandparents. One family may consist of three members, another may have fifteen. The variety of possibilities are numerous.

Second, families differ in structure. In a single-parent family the parent may be the authority figure. In a two-parent family father or mother may be the person in charge or they may share power and decision making. In another family where extended family is present a grandparent or some other relative may be the authoritative figure. The possibilities are many.

Third, families differ in communication patterns. In some families the expression of feelings is encouraged; in others the expression of cognitive thought is encouraged. One family may be rather quiet; another may be in a perpetual state of bedlam because everybody speaks at once. One family may be full of respectful listeners; whereas, in another family listening seems to be a lost art form.   Fourth, families differ in faith backgrounds and traditions. One family may have a long history within the Reformed tradition, another within the Wesleyan tradition. Still another family has an interfaith background with one parent coming from a Roman Catholic background and the other coming from the Nazarene church. Many varieties exist within individual churches as well.

Fifth, families vary with respect to where they are in the family cycle and with regard to the developmental stage of each of their family members. A young family is not an empty-nest family. A family with both teenagers and newborns is different from one with just teenagers. The possibilities are numerous.

The list of differences could be extended. However, our purpose here is not to present a comprehensive list, but to point out that differences like these affect the faith-nurturing needs of families. Painting the picture of faith for a three-member family will be quite different from painting the picture for a family of fifteen. The ways of nurturing faith will vary depending upon the denominational background of family members.

The point is that each family must find its own way of nurturing faith in God. There are no prepackaged faith-nurturing programs that are going to be appropriate for every family. To make such a claim would be to violate the integrity of any given family unit. Each family faces the challenge of finding those ways that help it create a meaningful family faith painting.

The Fine Strokes of Family Faith Nurturing

In this final section we want to consider some concrete methods and approaches that may be helpful in family faith nurturing depending on the uniqueness of each family. The suggestions come primarily from approaches we have found useful in our family; some are from other families who have told us about their ways of nurturing faith. There are many possible methods and approaches that have potential to accomplish qualitative faith nurturing if implemented in a context of love and trust. We have pointed to some ideas in examples given in previous chapters. Each family has to keep weaving together those methods that create a tapestry of faith nurturing for them.

Through the years we have tried and used many methods and approaches. The ones we describe here are among those that have been our favorites. Some come from our families of origin. The few we share from others' experiences were shared as having been favorites in other families. We hope some of these suggestions will be helpful to your family.

Sometimes in seeking methods for faith nurturing we adopt ideas directly from others. On other occasions an idea helps us to get started on creating an approach of our own which fits into our faith-nurturing approach more appropriately.

We have chosen to organize our suggestions according to the challenge we discussed in chapter 1. Our challenge to the family as a microcommunity of faith was to nurture its members in belonging, being, believing, benefiting, and becoming. You as the reader will notice that some of our suggestions could be listed under more than one category. We present them in catalogue fashion.

Belonging

Church attendance. We have stressed in our family the importance of worshiping with other members of the family of God. Our (Myron's and Jan's) ministry responsibilities sometimes require us to be away from our local church on Sundays. When our children were small, we negotiated whenever possible that one of us would be free to be with Mel and Tim in our home church. They grew to know the members of our congregation as the wider Christian family.

Special services of worship have become a particularly significant part of our family tradition. The Christmas Eve service and Maundy Thursday Communion have become part of our celebration during those holy seasons.

Church year. We have highlighted Advent, Christmas, Lent, and Easter as times when our family participates in special faith practices that unite us together as a family as well as with our larger Christian family.

During each season we have special devotionals. We trimmed a Jesse tree for several years during Advent. Our Advent devotional formats have been important, too. We light the candles on the Advent wreath. One of our humorous family memories is the time one year we learned a new Advent song. The first time through Jan played the autoharp and we all sang along more or less in tune. We reached the second line and Wootchie, our family dog, began to howl! We burst into laughter. The moment remains as a precious one in our memory banks. We keep an Advent calendar. Our major criteria in choosing one is that it must have some religious significance related to the birth of Jesus.

We have stressed that Christmas is a religious holy day. Our tree is decorated primarily with faith symbols. We have made many of the ornaments we use. Christmas music is special to all of us. We have incorporated it into our family life at a number of points. We have minimized the tradition of Santa Claus by referring to it as a game. We have several beautiful crèche decorations. We do not decorate with Santa Claus.

Before Lent two members of our family write half-page devotionals to be included in a booklet prepared by members of our church for congregational use. All four of us have contributed at one time or another. Last year we used a Lenten cross, lighting one of its candles on each Sunday. We decided it was a good experience in helping us as a family to focus on the meaning of Lent.

Easter for our family is a time of worship and celebration. We minimize bunnies, candy, presents, and new clothes. We greet each other in the morning with "He is risen. He is risen, indeed." The cross and spring flowers decorate our mantel and table on this special holy day.

Community prayer and music. Praying together as a family has been important to us. We join hands to pray together before the evening meal to show that we belong to one another and to God. This has been our practice for twenty-five years.

We have shared prayer during times of crises, both our own and others. We have prayed together at life's rituals and passages. Several families we know use their Christmas cards as an agenda for intercessory prayer during the first months of the year. Jan has personally prayed for the senders of cards as they come. We have discussed the idea of praying as a family for those persons after Christmas. We all affirm the idea, but we have yet to implement it.

Singing hymns, gospel choruses, and Christian folk songs has been one of our travel activities. We have covered many miles singing songs of faith as we go. At times we join to sing around the piano.

Listening to a wide range of Christian music on the stereo has been a shared activity. As Mel and Tim have grown older, they have begun to build their own tape and record collections. They have introduced us to some fine artists with challenging faith messages in music.

Conferences, camps, and retreats. We have found that attending conferences and camps with other Christian families helps us grow as a family unit and as individual persons. We have special memories of being together in California, Colorado, Maryland, Ohio, Pennsylvania, New York, and Wisconsin, sometimes for a week, sometimes for a weekend or an overnight.

We spent a week at the 1980 National Clown, Mime, Puppet, and Dance Ministry Workshop. The workshop had something in its program to interest and to involve each member of our family. The ecumenical nature of the conference provided a learning experience for us. Persons from a variety of religious persuasions were there to learn and to grow together. Our children had never before attended a Roman Catholic mass. The conference was also a shared experience in intergenerational faith learning.

Family history. We believe in passing the faith history of our family from one generation to another. Mel and Tim have heard about Myron's great grandfather being a "hard-shell Baptist" preacher. They have been told that their grandfather Chartier taught Sunday school. Jan's grandparents worshiped in the railroad chapel car before there was a church building. Today Mom Chartier is working on a grandmother's memory book. Our family history tells of the backgrounds of the faith pilgrims that make up our extended family.

Media and entertainment. We have attended movies and watched television specials that have presented aspects of faith in biblical times, in historical periods, or in the present. We don't always believe that these are accurately portrayed in every aspect, but we have found them informative and have often spent time together discussing them.

In our travels we have visited historical landmarks. Some of these have led to faith discussions about who we are as pilgrims in comparison with people of the past. Visits to New England have given us an opportunity to understand the Pilgrims and how religious freedom led them to the New World. In Lancaster County, Pennsylvania, we have compared our ways of being faith pilgrims with the ways of the Amish.

As a family we enjoy drama. This summer we attended productions of George Bernard Shaw's *Candida* and Henrik Ibsen's *Ghosts.* Both are social protest plays making strong statements about truth, established religion, and the clergy. We shared our viewpoints and feelings following these experiences.

Participative decision making. While some might not see family decision-making approaches as particularly faith oriented, we have found that how we make decisions has much to do with showing how we love and trust one another. We have worked at participative and collaborative styles that communicate that each person's opinions count and each one's needs are important. We have tried to show the importance of cooperation in helping our family reach its goals.

Some families have used the family council and attest to its importance to them. The council seems to do for them what we have worked out in other ways. It provides them with a structure.

Being

Baby dedication. (Baptism in some traditions.) We participated in services of dedication for both of our children. We took pictures of them and pressed flowers, which we mounted in their baby books along with the certificates of dedication. When the children were small, we looked at those pages many times and repeated the story that we had committed ourselves to raise them as persons having a faith identity related to Jesus Christ and his church.

Baptism. (Confirmation in some traditions.) At the time of their personal decisions for Christ, Mel and Tim were baptized. We planned to make these very special occasions. We have no extended family living close, so we gathered a group of close friends to be present at the service of worship and to join us for a luncheon of celebration in our home. Again we pressed the flowers to become part of their life-history mementos. We took pictures to record the event in which they declared their faith identity and commitment.

Candles of pilgrimage. We began at Mel's and Tim's baptism luncheons to light a special candle to commemorate on a yearly basis their growth in faith commitment and identity. We light Tim's on Palm Sunday and Mel's on Pentecost Sunday. These are the anniversaries of their baptisms.

Letters of pilgrimage. As our children have grown we have tried to write letters at important points of their life passages. The first letters we sent to Mel are recorded in her baby book. We wrote the most recent letters in April 1985, when she turned twenty-one. We will write others this year as she approaches college graduation. A part of our letters always includes our response to the faith pilgrimage that particular child is making.

When Tim was very ill, we told a close friend how concerned we were with Tim's condition. Not being a letter writer the friend sat down and recorded a tape in which he talked to Tim about how his faith had sustained him in difficult life periods. Tim's encounter with our friend by tape was one of the turning points of that long illness. Through listening to our friend's life story Tim took his own faith leap that God was truly present to empower him in those dark hours. This friend and his faith have had a deep impact upon Tim.

Personal prayer and devotion. We (Jan and Myron) believe in the power of prayer and in its importance to who we are as God's people. Each of us has cultivated a personal approach to God in prayer. We have encouraged Mel and Tim to find and practice their own ways. We began to model the importance of prayer through grace at meals and prayers at bedtime. As Mel and Tim grew we added other prayer experiences. Today they each use a daily guide to prayer and devotion. We (Myron and Jan) find our own approaches more fitting to our faith-pilgrimage stages.

Picture albums. As our family has moved through its life cycle, we have kept the camera busy. We have recorded many family and personal events. We have family picture books. Mel and Tim each have picture books. The pictures tell an important visual story of "being" development. Keeping them in order and up-to-date represents hours of work, but the result has been rich.

Believing

Bible reading. We (Myron and Jan) have our own practices with regard to Bible reading and study. We have participated in groups who have studied the Bible together. We keep working at our growth.

In our reading to Mel and Tim we began with very simple Bible story books. We chose small books with many colorful pictures which usually had one story. As they grew we added new Bible story resources. For a number of years we read a different children's Bible paraphrase each summer when all of us were less pressured with school. There are several fine paraphrases available. We purchased some; others we checked out of the church or the public library. The children enjoyed seeing the different pictures in the various books even though the stories sounded much the same. Now both Mel and Tim each own several versions of the Bible.

Discussion and sharing. We have talked about our faith beliefs on many occasions. The topics have varied over the years. Many of them have centered around Christian lifestyle and responsibility. The range of topics has been wide. Ecology, respect of others, peace and war, inclusive language, racism, simple lifestyle, affirmation of self, and sexual ethics are a few of the topics covered—some rather frequently. Such discussions have taken place in a number of settings: around the table, in the car, in the backyard, and with friends. Discussion has been one of our primary ways of faith nurturing. We engage in it with intensity in our family.

We also spend time sharing where we are as persons in our faith walk. When one person is sharing, the others primarily listen. Faith-sharing times are not used to express views and opinions, but rather to hear how another family member is experiencing the walk of faith at that time, and to hear how that member is putting his or her beliefs about God, the world, others, and self together. Sharing takes time spent together. We have budgeted that time on a regular basis for each member of our family.

Faith story reading. We (Jan and Myron) have appreciated reading biographies of persons of faith. Myron gave Jan a book on Mother Teresa as a special gift two years ago. He knew she would value it.

Mel and Tim have also done their share of reading about persons of faith. They have read about historical personalities such as Martin Luther as well as contemporary Christians like Charles Colson. Tim has particularly enjoyed books about Christian athletes. Mel has read broadly.

Interpreting symbols and practices. We (Jan and Myron) have always surrounded ourselves with symbols of the faith in our home. We have butterflies, fish, doves, and flowers in our living room. There is a silver cross commemorating our twenty-five years of marriage. As the children grew, we had opportunities to interpret to them the relevance of the symbols and their importance to us. In turn we have heard them explain the meaning of the symbols to their friends.

We have also tried to interpret our religious practices when the time seemed right. We have attempted to make theological explanations simple enough to be understandable yet complete enough to have substance.

Letters of faith. On the occasions of the baptisms of Mel and Tim we wrote to persons who lived at a distance and asked if they would write a letter of support and encouragement. We suggested that they might want to include a statement of what the Christian faith has meant to them. Both of them received beautiful letters supporting them in their initial steps as faith pilgrims and confessing the personal nature of the writer's faith. As their parents we were grateful for the time and effort family and friends invested in writing these faith epistles. Those letters have been read and reread by our children.

Sunday church school and other education settings. We (Myron and Jan) grew up attending Sunday church school. We have taught Sunday church school. We wanted to encourage our children to be part of a Sunday church school. We did that by searching out congregations that placed a high priority on Christian education. We also continued to attend rather than just send the kids.

Vacation Bible school and other church-sponsored summer programs have supplemented what we have taught at home. As Mel and Tim have grown older, they themselves have helped in teaching.

Mel and Tim attended a Christian high school which has had a deep impact on their belief structure. Their assignments have caused them to think deeply about their faith. Both of them had to explain seven views of creation. Then they had to articulate and elaborate on their own viewpoint. Both of them have had to address difficult topics related to Christian lifestyle. Mel wrote a Christian perspective paper on surrogate mothers, Tim wrote one on gambling. They have been challenged not to settle for easy answers.

Mel now continues her education at a Christian college. That setting of Christian higher education has challenged and nurtured her faith further.

Benefiting

Causes. Three causes in which our family has tried to be informed and take various kinds of action are world hunger, peace, and racism. We have tried to participate in church, school, and community-sponsored events when possible. We have contributed to these causes from our financial resources.

Family ministries. We have done some family ministry as clowns and with puppets. We see our contributions as small, but we are glad for the opportunities. Tim has become very serious in using puppetry to communicate the Christian faith. The rest of us have supported him.

In attending conferences we have met other families who have extensive ministries in music, puppetry, or clowning. We have learned from hearing their stories. These ministries have blessed others; they have also impacted the faith walks of these families.

Outreach. We have tried to be involved in outreach ministry when possible. Some or all of us have worked in soup kitchens, taught basic skills, led recreation, caroled in the city, shared our household supplies and clothing in the wake of area disasters, and donated food to an interfaith pantry.

Support ministries. We try to support our Christian brothers and sisters by reaching out to them. Some of our ways have been to provide meals, baby-sit, share our home, loan our car, make available ''personalized taxi'' transportation, give financial assistance, and mail cards and letters. In helping others much of the blessing has come to us.

Visitation. Perhaps visitation has a particular importance to us because we have had to deal with long-term illnesses and hospitalizations. Visitors who were sensitive to our conditions uplifted us and helped us feel concrete support. We have tried to be faithful in visiting shut-ins and in making brief contacts with those in hospitals. We have enjoyed making Christmas boxes filled with a variety of items at our church's Advent workshop. When our schedule has permitted, we have taken the box to a shut-in. When Tim was sick, one of the boxes came to our home. Our feelings were deep as evidenced by our teary eyes.

A family faith painting is continually in the process of becoming. Both broad strokes and fine strokes of faith nurturing have to be adjusted as families progress through various stages of family living. We constantly have to seek and to be open to the leading and empowering of God's Spirit as we seek to meet the challenge of nurturing faith in the family.

Our hope is that this book has been a stimulus for you and your family to be intentional about nurturing faith in the triune God. We wish you well as you seek to meet the challenge, to make the commitment to nurturing a family environment of trustworthy love, and to find your ways to nurture the faith of the various members of your family. God bless you in your endeavors together.

Questions for Reflection and Discussion

1. How well has your family done in creating a context of love and trust where persons are set free for faith and growth? In what areas could you improve?

2. To what extent have the modeling and mirroring educational approaches already become part of your family's way of living and of nurturing trust in God?

3. How would you identify the uniqueness of your family? How are you different from other families?

4. What fine-stroke methods of faith nurturing is your family currently doing? What new ideas did you obtain from this chapter that you'd like to try?

5. How do you sense that the Spirit of God is leading you in the challenge of nurturing faith in your family?

Notes

Chapter 1
The Challenge of Faith Nurturing

[1] M. Scott Peck, *The Road Less Traveled: A New Psychology of Love, Traditional Values and Spiritual Growth* (New York: Simon and Schuster, 1978), p. 15.

[2] Jerry M. Lewis, *How's Your Family?: A Guide to Identifying Your Family's Strengths and Weaknesses* (New York: Brunner/Mazel Inc., 1978), p. 170; Jerry M. Lewis and John G. Looney, *The Long Struggle: Well-Functioning Working-Class Black Families* (New York: Brunner/Mazel Inc., 1983), pp. 93, 106-107, 112-114, 138-139; David H. Olson *et al.*, *Families: What Makes Them Work* (Beverly Hills, Calif.: Sage Publications Inc., 1983), pp. 111-162.

[3] Olson *et al.*, *Families*, pp. 141-152.

[4] Dolores Curran, *Traits of a Healthy Family: Fifteen Traits Commonly Found in Healthy Families by Those Who Work with Them* (Minneapolis: Winston Press Inc., 1983), pp. 217-229; Lewis and Looney, *The Long Struggle*, pp. 71, 89, 106-108, 112, 138-139; Nicholas Stinnett, "Strong Families: A Portrait," in David Mace, ed., *Prevention in Family Services: Approaches to Family Wellness* (Beverly Hills, Calif.: Sage Publications Inc., 1983), pp. 27-38.

[5] Herbert Lingren *et al.*, "Enhancing Marriage and Family Competencies through Adult Life Development," in *Family Strengths 4: Positive Support Systems*, ed. Nick Stinnett *et al.* (Lincoln: University of Nebraska Press, 1982), pp. 385-386.

[6] Stinnett, "Strong Families," pp. 34-35.

[7] Jan and Myron Chartier, *Trusting Together in God: Living Your Faith, My Faith, and Our Faith* (St. Meinrad, Ind.: Abbey Press, 1984). See pp. 21-32 for a thorough discussion on the nature of faith.

[8] "Family Church Attendance: A Key to Evangelizing Future Generations," *The United Methodist Reporter*, December 1983.

Chapter 2
Commitment to Faith Nurturing

[1] H. Richard Niebuhr, *The Purpose of the Church and Its Ministry: Reflections on the Aims of Theological Education* (New York: Harper and Row, Publishers, Inc., 1956), p. 31.

[2] David R. Mace, *Close Companions: The Marriage Enrichment Handbook* (New York: Continuum Publishing Corp., 1982). See his discussions in chapters 1 and 2.

[3] We want to thank our former colleague, D. George Vanderlip, for helping us understand the theological significance of being children of God particularly as presented in Johannine literature.

[4] For stimulating and expanding our thinking on God's covenant with humanity, we want to thank our colleague, Manfred T. Brauch, who graciously granted us permission to attend his lectures in the course Theology of Marriage and Family.

[5] James W. Fowler, *Stages of Faith: The Psychology of Human Development and the Quest for Meaning* (San Francisco: Harper and Row, Publishers, Inc., 1981), p. xiii.

[6] "Playing Both Mother and Father," *Newsweek* (July 15, 1985), pp. 42-43.

[7] Dennis B. Guernsey, *A New Design for Family Ministry* (Elgin, Ill.: David C. Cook Publishing Co., 1982), pp. 23-25.

[8] J. Deotis Roberts, *Roots of a Black Future: Family and Church* (Philadelphia: The Westminster Press, 1980).

Chapter 3
God's Love—A Model for Faith Nurturing

[1] Gordon E. Jackson, "How Faith Is Formed" (Unpublished lectures delivered at the Northeast Continuing Education Event for American Baptist Ministers, Wagner College, Staten Island, N.Y., June 27-28, 1978).

[2] This discussion on the Trinity is based upon Jurgen Moltmann's *The Trinity and the Kingdom* (San Francisco: Harper and Row, Publishers Inc., 1981), pp. 171-178, 197-200.

[3] Henri J. M. Nouwen, "Care and the Elderly" (Unpublished lecture delivered at the biennial luncheon of the Ministers and Missionaries Benefit Board of the American Baptist Churches, U.S.A., Atlantic City, N.J., June 25, 1975).

[4] Frank Friedlander, "Alternative Modes of Inquiry," *Small Group Behavior*, no. 13 (1982), pp. 428-440.

[5] Erich Fromm, *The Art of Loving* (New York: Bantam Books Inc., 1956), p. 24.

[6] Victor Paul Furnish, *The Love Command in the New Testament* (Nashville: Abingdon Press, 1972), p. 210.

Chapter 4
Nurturing Love in the Family

[1] James R. Hine, *What Comes After You Say, "I Love You?"* (Palo Alto, Calif.: Pacific Books, Publishers, 1980); Floyd and Harriet Thatcher, *Long Term Marriage: A Search for the Ingredients of a Lifetime Partnership* (Waco, Tex.: Word Inc., 1980).

[2] Evelyn and Paul Moschetta, *Caring Couples* (Farmingdale, N.Y.: Coleman Publishing, Inc., 1984), Introduction.

Chapter 5
Developing Trustworthy Relationships in the Family

[1] This translation of Deuteronomy 7:9 is cited in Ignace de la Potterie, "Truth," in *Dictionary of Biblical Theology*, rev. ed. (New York: The Seabury Press, Inc. 1973), p. 618.

[2] James R. Hine, *How to Have a Long, Happy, Healthy Marriage* (Danville, Ill.: The Interstate Printers and Publishers, Inc. 1985), p. vii. See also Thatcher, *Long Term Marriage* (Waco Tex.: Word Inc., 1981), pp. 197-198 for the importance of faith and confidence in the marital process to a happy marriage.

[3] Hine, *What Comes After You Say*, pp. 42-43.

[4] *Ibid.*, pp. 61-62.

[5] Curran, *Traits*, pp. 17-24, 31-97.

[6] *Ibid.*, p. 99.

[7] J. Eugene Wright, Jr., *Erikson: Identity and Religion* (New York: The Seabury Press, Inc. 1982). pp. 148-178.

[8] Jack R. Gibb, *Trust: A New View of Personal and Organizational Development* (La Jolla, Calif.: Omicron Press, 1978), p. 19.

[9] *Ibid.*, p. 149.

[10] Jackson, "How Faith Is Formed"

[11] David W. Johnson, *Reaching Out: Interpersonal Effectiveness and Self-Actualization*, 2d ed. (Englewood Cliffs, N. J.: Prentice-Hall, Inc., 1981), p. 50.

[12] Bobby R. Patton and Kim Giffin, *Interpersonal Communication in Action: Basic Text and Readings*, 2d ed. (New York: Harper and Row, Publishers Inc., 1977), p. 368.

[13] In some cultures eye contact is perceived as offensive behavior; it does anything but contribute to trust.

[14] Carolyn Gratton, *Trusting: Theory and Practice* (New York: Crossroad Publishing Co., 1982), pp. 4-5.

[15] Gibb, *Trust*, p. 13.

Chapter 6
Faith Nurturing and the Individual Family Member

[1] James W. Fowler, *Stages of Faith: The Psychology of Human Development and the Quest for Meaning* (San Francisco: Harper and Row, Publishers Inc., 1981); John H. Westerhoff, III, *Will Our Children Have Faith?* (New York: The Seabury Press, Inc., 1976); Lewis Joseph Sherrill, *The Struggle of the Soul* (New York: The Macmillan Company, Inc., 1952); Wayne E. Oates, *On Becoming Children of God* (Philadelphia: The Westminster Press, 1969); Ron DelBene with Herb Montgomery, *The Hunger of the Heart* (Minneapolis: Winston Press, Inc., 1983). Rather than formulating their own conceptual frameworks, scholars have gained their insights into faith stages by using general models of human development and relating them to the specific area of faith. Erik Erickson's eight stages of human life have been used rather widely.

[2] For an example built from Erikson's thinking, see John J. Gleason, Jr., *Growing Up to God: Eight Steps in Religious Development* (Nashville: Abingdon Press, 1975). Jean Piaget's stages of cognitive thinking have also proven productive. For an example, see two books by Ronald Goldman, *Religious Thinking from Childhood to Adolescence* (New York: The Seabury Press, Inc. 1964) and Harold Loukes, *Readiness for Religion* (New York: The Seabury Press, Inc., 1965).

Chapter 7
Faith Nurturing and the Cycle of Family Life

[1] Rueben Hill and Roy H. Rodgers, "The Developmental Approach," in *Handbook of Marriage and the Family,* ed., Harold T. Christensen (Chicago: Rand McNally and Company, 1964), pp. 171-211.

[2] See three recent books on marriage and family life cycles. Elizabeth A. Carter and Monica Orfanidis, eds., *The Family Life Cycle: A Framework for Family Therapy* (New York: Halsted Press, 1980); David H. Olson, *et al., Families: What Makes Them Work* (Beverly Hills, Calif.: Sage Publications, Inc., 1983); Laura J. Singer, *Stages: The Crises That Shape Your Marriage* (New York: Grosset & Dunlap, 1980).

Chapter 8
Finding Your Way in Family Faith Nurturing

[1] These approaches are attributed to Albert Bandura and R. H. Walters, *Social Learning and Personality Development* (New York: Holt, Rinehart and Winston, Inc., 1963).

Suggestions for Further Reading

The following list of books and periodicals are offered as suggestions for further reading in family living and faith nurturing.

Books

Boyer, Ernest, Jr., *A Way in the World: Family Life as Spiritual Discipline*. San Francisco: Harper & Row, Publishers Inc., 1984.
This book is about the spirituality of the family. The author sees two kinds of spirituality—that of the secluded solitary life of contemplation and that of the family in the world of human relationships. He explores what each has to offer and how they can be joined.
Chartier, Jan and Myron, *Trusting Together in God: Living Your Faith, My Faith, and Our Faith*. St. Meinrad, Ind.: Abbey Press, 1984.
This book is designed to help married couples discover and nurture a shared faith. Through essays on important relational themes, structured exercises, and meditations, the nature of a shared faith is explored.
Chartier, Jan and Myron, gen. eds., Judson Family Life Series. Valley Forge: Judson Press, 1984-1986.
This series of books makes a contribution to understanding family dynamics from the Judeo-Christian perspective. Through implementing the counsel of these authors families can nurture health and faith. Books already published in the series are listed behind the title page of this book.
Curran, Dolores, *Traits of a Healthy Family: Fifteen Traits Commonly Found in Healthy Families by Those Who Work with Them*. Minneapolis: Winston Press, Inc., 1983.

This award-winning book is essential reading for any person concerned about the health and well-being of his or her family. Curran discusses how families can realistically foster fifteen traits chosen by family professionals as marks of healthy families.

Sawin, Margaret M. ed., *Hope for Families: Stories of Family Clusters in Diverse Settings.* New York: William H. Sadlier, Inc., 1982.

If you would like to nurture your family's faith with the help of other families, this book is recommended. Sawin, the founder of the family-cluster model in religious education, provides a compilation of case studies about family clusters in diverse settings. Through them she shows how family systems are impacted, how the group process develops, and how faith is inherent in the family cluster.

Westerhoff, John H., III, *Bringing Up Children in the Christian Faith.* Minneapolis: Winston Press, Inc., 1980.

This book presents sound ways for parents and children to grow together in the Christian faith. Practical suggestions on praying, celebrating, communicating, telling Bible stories, and performing acts of service and witness together are provided.

Periodicals

Marriage and Family Living is a monthly publication of Abbey Press. Its editorial purpose is to heal, support, enrich, and celebrate marriage and family relationships by offering sound advice of professionals and the experience of ordinary families in light of Gospel teaching. The address is *Marriage and Family Living,* St. Meinrad, IN 47577.

Festivals is published six times a year to bring the richness of the Christian tradition and ritual into the home. Articles, book reviews, calendars, and recipes are included. Write to *Festivals,* 160 E. Virginia Street #290, San Jose, CA 95112 for information and a sample copy.

The two recommended periodicals are published by Roman Catholic groups; both are quite useful to the larger ecumenical church and its families.